E.S. Reddy joined the United
Nations Secretariat as a Political
Officer in 1949. He was Political
Officer with the United Nations
Emergency Force in Egypt in
1956-57. He was appointed Principal
Secretary to the UN Special
Committee against Apartheid, when
it was established in 1963 and had
since been in charge of "apartheid"
in the United Nations Secretariat.
He became Director of the Centre
against Apartheid in 1967, with
responsibility for assisting the
Special Committee administering
funds for assistance to victims of
apartheid and promoting the
international campaign against
apartheid.

Reddy accompanied Major-General
Joseph Garba, Chairman of the
Special Committee, on missions to
many capitals and organized
numerous conferences against
apartheid. He was Executive
Secretary of the World Conference
for Action against Apartheid
(Lagos, August 1977) and of the
International Conference for
Sanctions against South Africa
(Paris, May 1981).

Though retired from service, he
lives in New York writing books on
South Africa and editing books on
Krishna Menon and Olof Palme.

OLIVER TAMBO
AND THE STRUGGLE
AGAINST APARTHEID

OLIVER TAMBO
AND THE STRUGGLE
AGAINST APARTHEID

Oliver Tambo addressing the U.N. 1982

Oliver Tambo
And The Struggle
Against Apartheid

Edited by

E. S. Reddy

Distributed By
APT BOOKS, INC.
141 East 44 Street
New York, N.Y. 10017

STERLING PUBLISHERS PRIVATE LIMITED
in collaboration with
NAMEDIA FOUNDATION

STERLING PUBLISHERS PRIVATE LIMITED

L-10, Green Park Extension, New Delhi 110016
G-2, Cunningham Apartments, Cunningham Road,
Bangalore 560052

ISBN: 81 207 0779 6

OLIVER TAMBO AND THE STRUGGLE
AGAINST APARTHEID

© 1987 E. S. Reddy

PRINTED AND PUBLISHED IN INDIA

Published by S. K. GHAI, Managing Director, Sterling Publishers Private
Limited, New Delhi and printed at Shaheed Prakashan Press, A 794,
Amar Puri, Pahar Ganj, New Delhi 110055.

CONTENTS

PREFACE

The struggle of the people of South Africa for the liquidation of the barbaric apartheid system is a saga of indomitable courage and unflinching determination. Its shining record of unflagging valour coincides with the entire length of the twentieth century as its vanguard detachment, the African National Congress, celebrates its 75th anniversary this year. This is a remarkable organ of struggle, perhaps unique in history. As the spearhead of the crusade against racial discrimination, it unifies within its ranks and also in its leadership three streams, the African, the Indian and the European, a symbol of the democracy, that it has been striving to achieve, replacing the hated apartheid regime.

The struggle of the people of South Africa and Namibia under the leadership of the African National Congress and the South West African People's Organisation has evoked worldwide solidarity, from all continents and every nation, cutting across barriers of race and creed, ideological differences, social and political systems. In this mighty crusade of humanity, millions are actively engaged today all over the world, men and women, young and old. The fight of the heroic people within the vast prison camp of apartheid has been orchestrated with the sustained movement of common people in all corners of the earth as a living symbol of unbroken solidarity with the freedom-fighters in South Africa. This is a unique feature of this struggle, which is today engaged in overpowering the desperate, last-ditch resistance of the perpetrators of despicable apartheid.

We, in India, have a special organic link with the heroic struggle against apartheid. It was in South Africa that the grand architect of our national struggle for freedom from British rule, Mahatma Gandhi, first experimented with his technique of non-violent mass movement, as he raised the banner against racial discrimination, before he came to India. India was the first country, that imposed economic sanctions against South Africa as early as 1946. Since then, the South African people's struggle against apartheid has always been regarded in India as very much a part of our own struggle for freedom, and today a continuation of it, as our national leaders have always enjoined that freedom is indivisible. Until the last bastion of apartheid falls in South Africa, the injunction of our own freedom will not be regarded as having been carried out in full.

The editor of this volume, Enuga S. Reddy, has been an intrepid champion of the struggle of liberation in Southern Africa for four decades now. His record of single-minded dedication to the cause is internationally acknowledged and his never-failing interest in it goes much beyond his record of activities in the capacity of the Director of the UN Centre against Apartheid, holding the post of an Assistant Secretary General of the United Nations. This volume bears testimony to his vast knowledge, experience and commitment to the struggle against apartheid, which he has been actively championing uptil this day.

Adhering to its objective of focussing the media interest on issues of freedom, non-alignment, justice and peace, NAMEDIA Foundation organised a seminar on "Media and the Struggle Against Apartheid" in New Delhi in May this year. It was attended by a wide spectrum of Indian media professionals together with well-known media personalities from the Frontline States, as also leading spokesmen of the ANC and SWAPO. The statement issued at the conclusion of the seminar was meant not only as an expression of the solidarity of the Indian people with those engaged in the struggle against the racist regime in Pretoria, but also an appeal for the greater activisation of the media in our country to focus on that struggle underlining its worldwide significance.

As part of its commitment of solidarity with the struggle against apartheid, the NAMEDIA Foundation is happy to be associated with the publication of this volume. It is being released on the 70th birthday of Oliver Tambo, President of the African National Congress. This volume is presented to him on this happy occasion as a modest token of our esteem and admiration for one of the great sons of the mighty African people.

NIKHIL CHAKRAVARTTY

New Delhi   *Chairman*
October 27, 1987   *NAMEDIA FOUNDATION*

सत्यमेव जयते

PRIME MINISTER

MESSAGE

The persistence of the system of apartheid in South
Africa constitutes both an anachronism in an era of
progressive emancipation and an affront to the
conscience of humankind. Concerted international
efforts to seek a peaceful end to this manifestation
of racism are being adamantly thwarted. The only
alternative left to South African patriots is to wage
a liberation movement. The African National Congress, which was founded seventy-five years ago, has
been the prime liberation movement engaged in
this challenging endeavour. It has been inspired in
its activities by the outstanding leadership qualities
of such distinguished patriots as Nelson Mandela
and Oliver Tambo. The seventy-fifth anniversary of
the establishment of the ANC is, thus, an event of
international significance and the decision to bring
out this publication has been timely. While the
ANC enjoys the unstinted support of all South
African patriots, there is a continuing need to
mobilise world public opinion against the evils of

apartheid and to bring about wider understanding of the consequences of allowing the repressive racist minority regime to rule the roost in South Africa. This publication will undoubtedly contribute towards this objective.

India has been in the forefront of the struggle against apartheid. Apart from our nation- endeavours to demand the establishment of a de[...]o- cratic polity in South Africa, we are committe[...] through our Chairmanship of the AFRICA Fund to assist the Southern African liberation movemen[...]n and the ANC in particular and to mobilise world public opinion against apartheid. It is our firm conviction that these combined efforts will culmi- nate in victory for the forces seeking freedom and dignity for the people of South Africa. Oliver Tambo is an eloquent spokesman of these forces. My wish for him on his 70th birthday, which falls next month, is that he should soon see the flag of freedom flying in South Africa.

RAJIV GANDHI

New Delhi
September 28, 1987

ALAS AFRICA...!

RABINDRANATH TAGORE

I.. n insane time, the long long past
   when the Creator himself
   gravely displeased with himself,
      destroyed his own creations
   over and over again,
the ocean with its angry arms snatched,
away a piece of eastern earth, and
   called it Africa....

Alas! Africa of shadows,
   your human face remains unknown,
to the uncaring game of blue Westerners.

They came:
   Human hunters all.
   The iron chains,
and claws sharper than those of wolves.
Their pride blinder than your sunless forests.

The barbaric lust of civilised men
   revealed in ugliness
of their own
   Inhumanity.

HOMAGE TO THE SPEARHEAD

MULK RAJ ANAND

Oliver Tambo!

Hero of Heroes of the struggle against Boer barbarism in South Africa!

Hero of the World, where some men and women believe that we can resist the overwhelming forces of tyranny!

Upholder of the dignity of men and women, of every colour, race and religion!

Inveterate fighter for liberty for your people — and therefore for all peoples!

Symbol of the Black people's hope that the Rights of Man will be recognised everywhere!

Faithful to the memory of those, who have perished in the fight against Apartheid!

I salute you on behalf of the many witnesses of your persistent actions in the struggles to right the wrongs!

You have worked for half a century without caring for applause!

You have acted without any sense of glory in obscure areas of your land!

You have not allowed yourself to be shaken in your faith that freedom will come, inspite of all the merciless suppression by the monstrous fascist-racist state power of the South African White usurpers of the vast lands of your peoples!

While the Western intelligentsia, in the cafes of London and New York, were talking of the need to act, in a world where they said "Hell is other people," you and your colleagues, Nelson Mandela, Yusuf Dadoo, Monty Naicker, Trevor Huddleston, Steve Biko, and many others, seized the Truth of Mahatma Gandhi and adopted *Satyagraha*, non-violent, non-cooperation.

But, when you saw that the passive resisters were trodden under the hoofs of policemen's horses, when you knew that the Boers considered the Blacks to be sons of Cain, to be enslaved, lower creatures, who must not be seen or heard, though they must work for the Whites, whose touch was supposed to defile them, whom they considered to be a mad mob every time they got together to assert their rights—you decided, with your millions of comrades to fight with whatever means might become available.

Mahatma Gandhi's stipulation that means are ends, you saw, can be a valid dictum, when those who oppose have a sense of moral law. But for two hundred years or more, the Boers have practised the Calvinist heresy to condemn the coloured people as vermin. They usurped the lands of the Blacks, appropriated the gold and the diamonds of your beloved earth, and condemned your people as "animals beyond the law." They organised apartheid, apartness, with devilish ingenuity, so as to consign the Black people to filthy ghetoes, while they lived on the fat of the land in roomy mansions. Truly, they have worked out, with the evil genius of Mephistopheles, laws and rules, with care of detail, to organise discriminations, so that millions of men and women and children live in the fantastic "hell in the sunshine," where once nature's bounty was for the sustenance of human beings.

Terror stalks the veld. There is nowhere the rebel can rest his head. The patriots have taken to the jungles. The Nazi norms apply. The state power, helped by the money power of accretive Western cousins is omnipotent. Black worker's rights are smashed up by the biggest police force in the world! Each

3

protest by the people is met with grapeshot! Every year sees a new Sharpeville! Every protest means intenser deprivation of the protesters! No one can go across the boundaries of rejection in a city street! No pity for pregnant women, who might forget their pass at home!

The Calvinist God has abolished Jesus of the Cross. In the name of their own Christ, they wage unending war, not only on the Black, Brown and Coloured People, but against all the peoples in the neighbouring States, which have won their freedom from the White yoke.

You, as the head of the African National Congress, deputising for Nelson Mandela, incarcerated for 25 years in an island jail, lead the patriotic strugglers against the unending war of a relentless enemy.

You and your comrades defy Death, the possible end, because you believe in the battle for freedom. Everyday is a new beginning for your comrades.

Of the two choices, the life of ease and the life of struggles so that you will not be slaves, but free human beings, you and your people have chosen to act rather than bear the living death of resting back.

You and your people have accepted hunger and want to achieve that immaterial thing called Liberty, which is the spirit in our flesh, and which demands, not the satisfaction of senses but sacrifice of every physical need. You know that the body is not mere physique but body-soul, where the will is nourished, so that men and women may become more than themselves, gods. You and your people have shown in your sustained struggle the capacity to bear pain, privation and face the onslaughts, daily, inspite of the fallen around you, inspite of the children howling from their derangement through seeing the torture of their parents.

There is no way back. There are only the tracks in the jungles, sinuous pathways of the struggle for freedom, onto the high roads.

Some of us, in our own vast land, heard the words of Jawaharlal

4

Nehru, in moments when everything seemed dark under the blanket of oppression of alien rule:

"All my life and all my strength are given to the first cause of the world: the liberation of mankind."

You will say the same words yourself till victory is achieved.

As you know, your enemies are divided, inwardly if not outwardly, because their centres cannot hold, from the anarchy loosed among them, by competition in the greed for more goods than others.

In your unity, the togetherness, which you have cemented among your people, along with your brother heroes and sister heroines, in the power of your joint will for freedom, is the hope for the future, when your land will receive you back as liberators, who will abolish rejection of one person by another.

Against rejection your will to power can never fail!

I salute you, as one of the men of hope against despair!

OLIVER TAMBO : A TRIBUTE

E.S. REDDY

In many colonial and social revolutions, the leaders of the people have had to go into exile to guide the resistance—or were imprisoned or deported—but continued to inspire their peoples in struggle.

The revolution in South Africa is, perhaps, unique in that the leadership and inspiration have been provided in a protracted struggle by a triumvirate in exile and prison: Oliver Tambo, President of the African National Congress, who has been in exile since 1960, while Nelson Mandela and Walter Sisulu have been in prison since 1962 and 1963 respectively after short periods in the underground.

The ANC has a tradition of collective leadership and significant contributions have been made to the movement by many others — such as Chief Albert Lutuli, J.B. Marks, Moses Kotane and Dr. Yusuf Dadoo — but the continuity of leadership provided by Tambo, Mandela and Sisulu has been crucial.

Oliver Tambo, who will be 70 on October 27, 1987 has borne the burden of guiding the resistance and securing international support for a quarter century. But his political life is inseparable from that of his two closest colleagues.

The three men joined the movement during the Second World War, when African youth raised the slogan "Quit Africa", in the wake of the "Quit India" movement led by Gandhiji, and were among the founding members of the ANC Youth League in 1944. The League exposed African freedom rather than a

6

mere mitigation of White racist oppression and mass action, instead of petitions and deputations to the racist rulers.

The Youth Leaguers were able in 1949, to secure the adoption by the ANC of their "positive action programme" of demonstrations and strikes, and even civil disobedience. Walter Sisulu became Secretary-General of ANC, while Oliver Tambo and Nelson Mandela were elected to the national executive.

The formulation of the strategy of the struggle was, however, not easy. For, South Africa was not a colony since Britain transferred power to the White settlers in 1910, but a country with a system of "internal colonialism." The Whites, the Coloured People and the Indians constituted a quarter of the population—and the Blacks constituted the majority three-quarters of the population. The task was not to oblige an external colonial power to leave but to secure transfer of power from a White minority regime to all the people.

The small Indian community had carried on a great passive resistance campaign against discrimination from 1946 to 1948, and had attracted the participation of a few Africans, the Coloured and Whites in solidarity with them. Dr. Yusuf Dadoo and Dr. G.M. Naicker, who had emerged as its leaders, declared that the freedom of the Indians was inextricably linked with the freedom of the African majority and advocated united resistance by all the oppressed people, as well as democratically minded Whites under African leadership.

The Government of India, led by Pandit Jawaharlal Nehru, made it clear that it sought no special privileges for Indians and promoted international support for the African cause as much as for the rights of the Indians.

The turning point in the South African struggle came in 1950, when the ANC, especially its militant young leaders, became convinced of the need for a united multi-racial struggle against the tyranny of apartheid. After extensive discussions and preparations, the ANC and the South African Indian Congress jointly launched the Defiance Campaign — a Satyagraha — in 1952, in which over 8,000 people of all racial origins courted imprisonment. Congresses of Coloured and White people and a multi-racial South African Congress of Trade Unions were formed and became part of the "Congress Alliance." They accepted as their common programme the Freedom Charter, formulated by an impressive multi-racial conference in June, 1955, proclaiming that South Africa belonged to all its people and pledging to struggle jointly for the total elimination of racial discrimination.

Walter Sisulu, as Secretary-General of ANC, played a crucial role in organizing the Defiance Campaign and other joint actions. Nelson Mandela was the Volunteer-in-Chief of the Defiance Campaign. Oliver Tambo led the campaigns against the forcible eviction of African communities and the imposition of the "Bantu education" system. He also played an important role in forging the united front.

As the rulers escalated repression to suppress non-violent resistance, the ANC leadership expected the banning of the organization and mass arrests of its members. It decided that one of the leaders should go abroad to mobilize international support and action. Oliver Tambo, who had been elected to a newly-created post of Deputy President, when restriction orders were served on the President-General of the ANC, Chief Albert Lutuli, was persuaded to undertake this task.

Tambo escaped from South Africa in April, 1960, together with Dr. Yusuf Dadoo, President of the South African Indian Congress and Ronald Segal, a well-known White journalist. The Indian Government helped them with travel documents and facilities to go to London to meet Commonwealth leaders. Tambo and Dadoo then visited Delhi for full discussions with Pandit Nehru, which led to the forcing out of South Africa from the Commonwealth and other international initiatives.

Meanwhile, in May, 1961, a national strike against the establishment of a White racist republic — led by Nelson Mandela from the underground — was suppressed by a massive show of military power.

Tambo immediately organized a secret conference of leaders of ANC and its allies in Bechunaland and it decided that an armed struggle had become imperative. The "Umkhonto we Sizwe"

8

("Spear of the Nation"), a multi-racial military wing, was founded under the leadership of Mandela. And, Tambo had to undertake the additional responsibility of arranging military training for its cadres. "Umkhonto we Sizwe" organised hundreds of acts of sabotage in the next two years, taking extreme care to avoid loss of life, in an effort to persuade the White minority to rethink and the international community to act.

The Pretoria regime responded with mass arrests of militants, who were well known and had little experience of clandestine activity. Through brutal torture and savage sentences under draconian laws, it was able to destroy the underground structures of the movement. Nelson Mandela was captured in August, 1962 and Walter Sisulu in July, 1963, and both were sentenced to life imprisonment in 1964. Chief Albert Lutuli was restricted to Groutville reserve and died in a mysterious accident in 1967.

It now fell to Oliver Tambo not only to promote international action but to ensure the restoration of the underground structures in South Africa and the revival of the struggle, both non-violent and violent, under the most difficult conditions. It is largely due to the respect enjoyed by him, his remarkable leadership and tireless efforts that the unity of the liberation movement was sustained and strengthened despite the serious reverses.

By the mid-1970's, the underground structures were re-established and made secure. Mass mobilization against apartheid reached unprecedented levels and armed struggle developed rapidly with thousands of young volunteers. Tens of thousands of people began to defy the law and virtually "unbanned" the ANC.

Nelson Mandela and Walter Sisulu remained in prison rejecting offers of conditional release, as symbols of the indomitable spirit of resistance. The movement found ways to keep them abreast of the struggle and they have truly contributed to the development of its strategy even from behind bars.

Tambo in exile and Mandela and Sisulu in prison have thus been the guiding spirits of a revolutionary upsurge involving people of varied racial origins and ideologies, and combining civil disobedience and armed struggle. The authorities are unable to suppress it despite the State of Emergency, the detentions of tens of thousands of people, mass torture of prisoners, even of children and murder of militants by vigilantes.

International solidarity, too, has advanced tremendously, though a few powerful governments continue to block decisive action and the anti-apartheid movement has become one of the most significant popular movements of our time.

Oliver Tambo has proved an outstanding leader of his people and has earned respect and admiration around the world as a "statesman-in-exile."

I met Oliver Tambo in 1960, soon after he escaped from south Africa, and have been closely associated with him and his family since I became the Principal Secretary of the United Nations Special Committee against Apartheid in 1963. His broad vision, deep attachment to democracy and non-racialism, tremendous integrity and personal warmth have been a source of inspiration to me. He is of the mould of the great leaders of the Indian struggle for freedom — and a sincere friend of India.

A brilliant student, teacher and lawyer — in association with Nelson Mandela he ran a legal firm — he sacrificed a promising career to lead the freedom movement. His long exile has been painful with his closest colleagues in prison and he had to resist the urge to be among his people as they fight a monstrous tyranny.

Tambo could spare little time to spend with his family — his wife, Adelaide, and their three daughters — or even to care for his own health, as the demands of the struggle have given him no respite.

A modest man, he has rejected all honours to himself — and accepted an honorary degree from the Jawaharlal Nehru University, New Delhi most reluctantly, while encouraging the world to honour Nelson Mandela, who is like a younger brother to him. Indeed, there was no one else to receive awards on behalf of Mandela like the Jawaharlal Nehru Award for International Understanding and the Third World Foundation Award to Nelson and Winnie Mandela.

But, the numerous friends around the world — whom he inspired and for whom he symbolizes the spirit and vision of the great freedom movement of South Africa — will find ways to pay tribute to him — like this book for instance.

OLIVER REGINALD TAMBO

BIOGRAPHICAL SKETCH

Born on October 27, 1917 at Bizana in Eastern Pondoland, Eastern Cape, and of peasant origin, he attended school at Ludebe, the Holy Cross Mission and later at St. Peter's Secondary School, Johannesburg. Matriculating in 1938, he went on to Fort Hare University College, where he graduated in 1941 with a B.Sc. degree. After being involved in students' strikes and expelled from Fort Hare, he obtained his Education Diploma and taught at St. Peter's Secondary School from 1943 to 1947, where his students included the late Duma Nokwe.

In 1948, he began studying law and started in legal practice with Nelson Mandela, who is now serving life imprisonment on Robben Island, in December 1952, establishing the first African legal partnership in South Africa.

He was one of the founders of the ANC Youth League in 1944, and successively its National Secretary and National Vice-President. In 1949, he became a member of the National Executive of the ANC and Secretary-General of the organisation in 1955, holding the position until 1958, when he was elected Deputy President General.

In 1954, he was served with government orders under the Suppression of Communism Act, banning him from attending all gatherings for two years and restricting his movements to the magisterial districts of Johannesburg and Benoni for the same period. In December, 1956 he was charged along with 155 other members of the Congress Alliance with High Treason. And in 1959, he was served with a further government order prohibiting him from attending any gatherings for a period of five years.

The legal practice, he and Nelson Mandela had set up as a means of defending Africans charged with "crimes" was seriously affected. He could not now travel to places like South West Africa (Namibia) as he had done before, to represent the Africans facing political charges and involved in political disputes with the government. A week after the Sharpeville shootings on March 21, 1960 and two days before the declaration of a State of Emergency on March 30, he was directed by the ANC National Executive to go out of the country in order to put the case against South Africa in world forums.

Tambo's role in arousing world consciousness has had an immense impact on international opinion about South Africa. Since coming out of South Africa in 1960, he has earned the respect of many world figures by his honesty, modesty, his incisive intelligence and his historic indictments against the South African regime at the United Nations and other world platforms. So ably has he presented the case against South Africa that he has come to be regarded as a man whose authority cannot be challenged on such issues. He has travelled widely. The esteem with which he is regarded in Africa can be judged by the fact that the movement he leads, the ANC, is regarded as the sole authentic and representative voice of the Black masses of South Africa. He knows personally almost all African leaders on the continent who have a great respect for his opinions. His speeches have been published and translated into many languages.

He is the President of the African National Congress (since 1967) and Chairman of the Political-Military Council.

THE STRUGGLE FOR A BIRTHRIGHT

FROM PLAATJE TO TAMBO:
FROM SEME TO MANDELA

The people of South Africa today are engaged in a desperate struggle to overthrow apartheid and reclaim their birthright. They have rejected the racism of the White minority rulers and the division of their country into different areas. They are determined to win back their national rights and to establish equal rights for all, the right to live and work without regard to race. Above all, they want to win their right to determine their own future and to choose their own government.

The African National Congress, the ANC, represents the authentic voice of all those in South Africa, who stand with them against the oppressor and for the rights of the oppressed. The struggle is not simply one for individual liberty, although it is true that individual liberties will not be won as long as apartheid lasts.

South Africa is unique in the world today in that the majority of its people have no vote and no means of control over their own lives; they are savagely exploited and their labour serves only to fuel the engines of profit for the apartheid system and their rulers. The White minority rulers function like the colonial rulers of past centuries, but with all the apparatus of a modern state, so that the machinery of repression is exceptionally strong and far-reaching.

It is, therefore, a tribute to the majority in South Africa that the struggle is not simply aimed at replacing a White minority regime by a Black majority one. It is a struggle for national

14

liberation, but it is also a struggle to rid the country of racism, to found a truly free and democratic South Africa in which all will have an equal right to live and work.

There is no doubt that the ANC is playing a pre-eminent role in this process. Its flag flies at funerals and demonstrations all over the country, its slogans are popular cries, the Freedom Charter, which was drawn up under its auspices, attracts ever greater support. Internationally, it has also received widespread recognition. The United Nations, the European Community, the Commonwealth, the NAM and many major world leaders (and significantly international big business) have stated that the unbanning of the ANC and the release of Nelson Mandela are an essential prelude to any serious efforts to end the terrible trauma of apartheid and avert the holocaust that threatens.

It is now 75 years since the ANC was founded. It is the oldest liberation movement in Africa. In the long hard years of struggle the ANC has grown to become a mature organisation, rich in experience, firmly dedicated to the principles of non-racism, and determined to build a new country, in which all will play their part and the welfare of all will be of equal concern.

To quote Thabo Mbeki, ANC Director of Information, UK, "We are all of us inspired by the confidence that victory is in sight. That is what accounts for the willingness of the people to engage in struggle every day, despite the shootings and the State of Emergency. It's because there is that great feeling that we are winning. We can't put a date on it but it's coming. Surely it must — soon."

HISTORY OF THE STRUGGLE

The African National Congress of South Africa was formed under the name of the "Native National Congress" in 1912. The Act of Union of 1910, the handing over by the British of the four different provinces of South Africa to a "Union" of Boer and British settlers, was seen by Africans as a betrayal. The Whites retained all their colonial powers over the non-Whites, and the way was paved for the Boers, descendants of the original 17th century Dutch settlers, who already outnumbered the English-speaking settlers among the White electorate, to take ultimate control.

It was in response to these events that on January 8, 1912, in Bloemfontein a massive conference was held of Africans from all areas. The purpose of the gathering was mainly to eliminate old tribal rivalries and to unite Africans against the injustices of the new system. A major grievance lay in the system, whereby Africans and only Africans, were obliged to carry identity papers, the forerunner of the hated Pass Laws.

A journalist, Solomon (Sol) Plaatje was elected Secretary and Pixley Ka Izaka Seme, a lawyer educated in New York and Oxford, become Treasurer. These leaders developed a programme of constitutional protest against the colour bar, which prevented Africans from taking any significant part in the political, administrative or economic life of the country. The Congress, with Sol Plaatje as its main spokesman, lobbied at the imperial government in London, in particular that the 1913 Land Act, which reserved more than 80 per cent of the land for 13 per cent of the population, should be scrapped. The British refused to disallow the legislation.

Following the First World War, the focus of resistance to White domination widened from the Pass Laws to include labour disputes and the ANC became closely associated with Clements Kadalie's Industrial and Commercial Workers' Union, which for a few years enjoyed huge support.

However, it was not until after World War II that the Congress itself attempted to organise the masses. The transformation was largely brought about through the new ANC Youth League, whose Secretary was Oliver Tambo; other prominent leaders were Walter Sisulu, Albertina Sisulu, and Nelson Mandela. The League put in train a "Programme of Action" to radicalise the movement.

In 1948, the hardline National Party came to power. Although the main basis of apartheid already existed in the form of the division of land (laid down formally in the 1913 Land Tenure Act), the Pass System and the voting system, Africans had not all previously been totally disenfranchised and many forms of segregation were traditional rather than legalyl enforced. The National Party set about institutionalising discrimination on grounds of colour.

This galvanised the ANC into adopting the Youth League's Programme of Action at its annual conference in 1949. The Defiance of Unjust Laws Campaign that followed (a campaign of mass protest, passive resistance and strikes) was led by the ANC and by the South African Indian Congress. Over 8,000 volunteers were trained and subsequently went to jail. It was not this however, that brought the campaign to a halt, but rather the vicious use of the Public Order Act to ban all support for the campaign, direct and indirect.

Under its new president elected in 1952, Chief Albert Lutuli, the ANC formulated a fresh strategy to implement a "positive programme for freedom." Activists consulted with their communities to gather the people's demands in preparation for a National Convention of all the people regardless of their race, creed or colour.

The ANC, the SAIC, the Congress of Democrats, formed by the Whites in 1952, the SA Coloured People's Organisation and the South African Congress of Trade Unions, formed in 1955, all united to organise the Congress of the People, which took place in June, 1955 in Kliptown, near Johannesburg. Three thousand delegates met to adopt the Freedom Charter, which remains to this day the essential basis of the ANC's campaign.

A year later the regime retaliated by arresting 156 leaders of all races, who were charged with high treason. Their trial lasted for four years — and ended with the release of all the accused. Meanwhile, however a group led by Robert Sobukwe had split from the ANC to form the Pan-Africanist Congress (PAC). They rejected cooperation with White activists.

The ANC had planned a National Anti-Pass Campaign to start in March, 1960, but it was at a PAC-organised anti-Pass demonstration in Sharpeville on March 21, that the police massacred 69 peacefully protesting Africans. Most of them were shot in the back, as they were running away. The ANC called a national strike and the mass burning of the Passes, but the regime panicked and announced a State of Emergency. Both the ANC and the PAC were declared illegal.

Up to that point the ANC had deliberately embraced a policy of peaceful resistance to the apartheid regime. One of the major philosophical influences on the ANC was provided by Mahatma Gandhi, who pioneered the use of passive resistance to achieve the goal of national liberation. Gandhi spent some years in South Africa, and was instrumental in forming the Natal Indian Congress in 1894. His ideas proved a powerful force and his son, Manilal, was prominent in the '50s Defiance Campaign. Although the State tried to pin charges of violence on the ANC, they could provide no proof.

Indeed, at the conclusion of the Treason Trial when all 156 accused were found not guilty. The Judge himself said that he accepted the "evidence that you (the ANC leaders) have consistently advised your followers to follow a peaceful course of action and to avoid violence in any shape or form."

This was internationally recognised, when Chief Albert Lutuli became the first Black person to be awarded the Nobel Prize for Peace in 1960.

However, with the increasing use of state terror to thwart the opponents of apartheid, and the banning of the movement, the ANC was compelled to reconsider its position. The National Party government had gradually closed off all the normal democratic avenues of protest, and nearly all forms of demonstration could be held to be illegal. Africans had no right to stand for parliament and no vote. In addition, the ANC leaders felt it would be wrong to continue to call for mass demonstrations, when they had no means of defending the people from indiscriminate slaughter by the police or the military.

After half a century of non-violent resistance, the ANC made the decision to form a military wing — "Umkhonto we Sizwe" (Spear of the Nation). MK, as it is now popularly known, declared itself on December 16, 1961 with the sabotage of various electric installations and government offices.

Nelson Mandela, its Commander, explained:

"The time comes in the life of any nation, when there

18

remains only two choices — submit or fight. That time has now come in South Africa. We shall not submit and we have no choice but to hit back by all means within our power in defence of our people, our future and our freedom."

Precisely the same decision was taken by the resistance in World War II, which concluded that Nazism had to be fought by all means available if it was to be defeated.

Umkhonto's initial campaign was one of sabotage, directed against government installations and key strategic places. It was a low-key campaign, which scrupulously avoided striking at people, and indeed the only human casualties were two of the saboteurs themselves.

That humane tradition continues up to the present day, and it is significant that in 1980, the ANC, at a ceremony at the headquarters of the International Red Cross, declared its adherence to the Geneva Conventions of 1949 and their Protocol of 1977 on the humanitarian conduct of war.

The apartheid regime itself has consistently refused to sign the Protocol.

But in July 1963, Walter Sisulu, Nelson Mandela, Govan Mbeki and the other major leaders of Umkhonto were all arrested at Rivonia and charged with sabotage and recruiting others for training in order to overthrow the State. A vast international campaign was launched to save them from an almost certain death penalty. The campaign succeeded in that eight of them were sentenced, not to death but to life imprisonment and sent to Robben Island, while the ninth, Lionel Bernstein was found not guilty.

The years that followed were difficult ones, but the struggle continued nonetheless. In 1967, the Lutuli Combat Cetachment comprising ANC and ZAPU guerillas crossed the Zambezi into Rhodesia, where they fought the Smith regime at Wankie and Sipolilo.

Then in the '70s the situation in Southern Africa changed dramatically. Angola and Mozambique won their freedom from the Portuguese, and inspired the Youth of South Africa. A new awareness of the value of Black culture and traditions, as new emphasis on the dignity of the Black person, found its expression in the Black Consciousness Movement. Another generation took to the streets in open opposition to apartheid and especially in rejection of teaching through Afrikans, seen as a symbol of their oppressors. In June, 1976 Soweto erupted, followed by townships throughout the country. June 16, 1976 is now known internationally as Soweto Day or Day of the Youth of South Africa.

Nearly 2,000 died, murdered by the regime, while thousands more fled the country to escape detention and torture. Jail conditions were highlighted by the death of the charismatic Black Consciousness leader, Steve Biko, battered to death by his prison warders. Black Consciousness organisations, some of which were beginning to engage in dialogue with the ANC, and Black newspapers, were closed down.

But new organisations soon sprang up to take their place, such as the Azanian People's Organisation, AZAPO. Debates raged over the future development of the whole Black Consciousness philosophy, which some saw as a stage, necessary but still only a stage, on the way to national liberation, while others viewed its radical exclusivity as desirable in itself. AZAPO has never received wide-spread support from workers.

Meanwhile, the inheritors of the proud ANC traditions, its non-racialism and the social aims of the Freedom Charter, were working to establish a new organisation. They were spurred on by the regime's plans to introduce a new Constitution (since brought into operation), which would set up separate Indian and Coloured chambers, in addition to the White Parliament.

In August, 1983, the United Democratic Front emerged. It is an umbrella organisation comprising over 600 organisations of all kinds -- church bodies, community and civic organisations, youth groups, trade unions, women's organisations and sporting and cultural groups. Its initial campaign for a boycott of the elections of the tricameral Parliament was an astounding success: in some constituencies only 2 per cent of the voters went to the polls, registering a heartening rejection of racist structures.

The establishment of the tricameral Parliament also sparked off a new wave of fury among the African majority, who were excluded even from this limited voice in affairs. Once more the townships erupted, while from the ANC came the call to render apartheid unworkable and the country ungovernable. Neither ferocious repression nor cosmetic reforms have stemmed this tide of opposition.

The first half of the decade of the '80s has made clear the huge support which the ANC enjoys in South Africa. Nelson Mandela and Oliver Tambo, the one still serving a life sentence and the other in exile, enjoy a greater prestige inside and outside their country than any other South African. The struggle is indeed being intensified at all levels.

As the Freedom Charter says, "The People Shall Govern!" But the day of victory will be hastened by continued international support for the ANC's campaign.

Freedom is Coming in South Africa!

Courtesy: Irish Anti-Apartheid Movement.

AFRICA AND FREEDOM

CHIEF ALBERT LUTULI'S NOBEL LECTURE

Chief Albert John Lutuli, the President-General of the African National Congress from 1952 to 1967 was the first Black African to be honoured with the Nobel Prize for Peace in 1961. Chief Lutuli was born in 1898 and brought up under tribal conditions like many other African leaders. He was not a hereditary Chief as his Zulu tribe had a democratic system of electing Chiefs.

He triumphed over them to become a bold and courageous patriot, a man of lofty principles and a statesman. On July 21, 1967, it was alleged that he was run over by a train. A true and practising Christian, he dedicated his life to the cause and service of his fellow South Africans. He was arrested and banned many times and he was deposed from chieftaincy, as he preferred to lead the ANC.

The following is the text of the Nobel Lecture delivered by Chief Lutuli on December 11, 1961.

In years gone by, some of the greatest men of our century have stood here to receive this Award, men whose names and deeds have enriched the pages of human history, men whom future generations will regard as having shaped the world of our time. No one could be left unmoved at being plucked from the village of Groutville, a name many of you have never heard before and which does not even feature on many maps — plucked from banishment in a rural backwater, lifted out of the narrow confines of South Africa's internal politics and placed here in the shadow of these great figures. It is a great honour to me to stand on this rostrum where many of the great men of our times have stood.

The Nobel Peace Award that has brought me here has for me a threefold significance. On the one hand, it is a tribute to my humble contribution to efforts by democrats on both sides of the colour line to find a peaceful solution to the race problem. This contribution is not in any way unique. I did not initiate the struggle to extend the area of human freedom in South Africa. Other African patriots—devoted men—did so before me! I also, as a Christian and patriot, could not look on while systematic attempts were made, almost in every departments of life, to debase the God-factor in Man or to set a limit beyond which the human being in his Black form might not strive to serve his Creator to the best of his ability. To remain neutral in a situation, where the laws of the land virtually criticised God for having created men of colour was the sort of thing I could not, as a Christian, tolerate.

On the other hand, the Award is a democratic declaration of solidarity with those who fight to widen the area of liberty in my part of the world. As such, it is the sort of gesture, which gives me and millions who think as I do, tremendous encouragement. There are still people in the world today, who regard South Africa's race problem as a simple clash between Black and White. Our government has carefully projected this image of the problem before the eyes of the world. This has had two effects. It has confused the real issues at stake in the race crisis. It has given some form of force to the government's contention that the race problem is a domestic matter for South Africa. This, in turn, has tended to narrow down the area over which our case could be better understood in the world.

From yet another angle, it is a welcome recognition of the role played by the African people during the last fifty years to establish, peacefully, a society in which merit and not race, would fix the position of the individual in the life of the nation.

This Award could not be for me alone, nor for just South Africa, but for Africa as a whole. Africa presently is most deeply torn with strife and most bitterly stricken with racial conflict. How strange then it is that a man of Africa should be here to receive an Award given for service to the cause of peace and brotherhood between men. There has been little peace in Africa in our time. From the nothernmost end of our continent, where war has raged for seven years, to the centre and to the south, there are battles being fought out, some with arms, some without. In my own country, in the year 1960 for which this Award is given, there was a State of Emergency for many months. At Sharpeville, a small village, in a single afternoon 69 people were shot dead and 180 wounded by small arms fire, and in parts like the Transkei, a State of Emergency is still continuing. Ours is a continent in revolution against oppression. And peace and revolution make uneasy bedfellows. There can be no peace until the forces of oppression are over-thrown.

Our continent has been carved up by the great powers; alien governments have been forced upon the African people by military conquest and by economic domination; strivings for nationhood and national dignity have been beaten down by force; traditional economics and ancient customs have been disrupted, and human skills and energy have been harnessed for the advantage of our conquerors. In these times, there has been no peace; there could be no brotherhood between men.

But now, the revolutionary stirrings of our continent are setting the past aside. Our people everywhere from north to south of the continent are reclaiming their land, their right to participate in government, their dignity as men, their nationhood. Thus, in the turmoil of revolution, the basis for peace and brotherhood in Africa is being restored by the resurrection of national sovereignty and independence, of equality and the dignity of man. It should not be difficult for you here in Europe to appreciate this.

Your continent passed through a longer series of revolutionary upheavals, in which your age of feudal backwardness gave way to the new age of industrialisation, true nationhood, democracy and rising living standards — the golden age for which men have striven for generations. Your age of revolution, stretching across all the years from the 18th century to our own, encompassed some of the bloodiest civil wars in all history. By comparison, the African revolution has swept across three quarters of the continent in less than a decade; its final completion is within sight of our own generation. Again, by comparison with Europe, our African revolution — to our credit, is proving to be orderly, quick and comparatively bloodless.

This fact of the relative peacefulness of our African revolution is attested to by other observers of eminence. Professor C. W. de Kiewiet, President of the Rochester University, U.S.A., in the Hoernle Memorial Lecture for 1960, has this to say: "There has, it is true, been almost no serious violence in the achievement of political self-rule. In that sense there is no revolution in Africa — only reform . . ."

Professor D. V. Cowen, former Professor of Comparative Law at the University of Cape Town, South Africa, in the Hoernle Memorial Lecture for 1961, throws light on the nature of our struggle in the following words: "They (the Whites in South Africa) are, again, fortunate in the very high moral calibre of the non-White inhabitants of South Africa, who compare favourably with any on the whole continent." Let this never be forgotten by those who so eagerly point a finger of scorn at Africa.

Perhaps, by your standards, our surge to revolutionary reforms is late. If it is so — if we are late in joining the modern age of social enlightenment, late in gaining self-rule, independence and democracy, it is because in the past the pace has not been set by us. Europe set the pattern for the 19th and 20th century development of Africa. Only now is our continent coming into its own and recapturing its own fate from foreign rule.

Though I speak of Africa as a single entity, it is divided in many ways — by race, language, history and custom; by political, economic and ethnic frontiers. But in truth, despite these multiple divisions, Africa has a single common purpose and a single goal — the achievement of its own independence. All Africa, both lands which have won their political victories, but have still to overcome the legacy of economic backwardness, and lands like my own, whose political battles have still to be waged to their conclusion — all Africa has this single aim; our goal is a united Africa, in which the standards of life and liberty are constantly expanding; in which the ancient legacy of illiteracy and disease is swept aside; in which the dignity of man is rescued from beneath the heels of colonialism which have trampled it. This goal, pursued by millions of our people with revolutionary zeal, by means of books, representations, demonstrations, and in some places armed force provoked by the adamancy of the White rule, carries the only real promise of peace in Africa. Whatever means have been used, the efforts have gone to end alien rule and race oppression.

There is a paradox in the fact that Africa qualifies for such an Award in its age of turmoil and revolution. How great is the paradox and how much greater the honour that an Award in support of peace and the brotherhood of man should come to one, who is a citizen of a country, where the brotherhood of man is an illegal doctrine, outlawed, banned, censured, proscribed and prohibited; where to work, talk or campaign for the realisation in fact and deed of the brotherhood of man is hazardous, punished with banishment or confinement without trial or imprisonment; where effective democratic channels to peaceful settlement of the race problem have never existed these 300 years; and where minority power rests on the most heavily armed and equipped military machine in Africa. This is South Africa.

Even here, where the White rule seems determined not to change its mind for the better, the spirit of Africa's militant struggle for liberty, equality and independence asserts itself. I, together with thousands of my countrymen, have in the course of the struggle for these ideals, been harassed, and imprisoned, but we are not deterred in our quest for a new age in which we shall live in peace and in brotherhood.

It is not necessary for me to speak at length about South Africa; its social system, its politics, its economics and its laws have forced themselves on the attention of the world. It is a museum piece in our time, a hangover from the dark past of mankind, a relic of an age, which everywhere else is dead or dying. Here, the cult of race superiority and of White supremacy is worshipped like a god. Few White people escape corruption and many of their children learn to believe that the White men are unquestionably superior, efficient, clever, industrious and capable;

26

that the Black men are, equally unquestionably, inferior, sloth-
ful, stupid, evil and clumsy. On the basis of the mythology
that "the lowest amongst us is higher than the highest
amongst them", it is claimed that White men build everything
that is worthwhile in the country; its cities, its industries, its
mines and its agriculture, and control these things, whilst
Black men are only temporary sojourners in these cities, fitted
only for menial labour, and unfit to share political power. The
Prime Minister of South Africa, Dr. Verwoerd, then Minister
of Bantu Affairs, when explaining his government's policy on
African education had this to say: "There is no place for him
(the African) in the European community above the level of
certain forms of labour."

There is little new in this mythology. Every part of Africa
which has been subject to White conquest has, at one time or
another, and in one guise or another, suffered from it, even in
its virulent form of the slavery that obtained in Africa up to the
19th century.

The mitigating feature in the gloom of those far-off days was the
shaft of light sunk by Christian missions, a shaft of light to
which we owe our initial enlightenment. With successive
governments of the time doing little or nothing to ameliorate
the harrowing suffering of the Black man at the hands of slave-
drivers, men like Dr. Livingstone and Dr. John Philip and
other illustrious men of God stood for social justice in the face
of overwhelming odds. It is worth noting that the names I
have referred to are still anathema to some South Africans.
Hence, the ghost of slavery lingers on to this day in the form of
forced labour that goes on in what are called farm prisons. But
the tradition of Livingstone and Philip lives on, perpetuated by
a few of their line. It is fair to say that even in present-day conditions, Christian missions have been in the vanguard of initiat-
ing social services provided for us. Our progress in this field
has been in spite of, and not mainly because of, the government.

In this, the Church in South Africa — though belatedly, seems
to be awakening to a broader mission of the Church, in its
ministry among us. It is beginning to take seriously the words

of its Founder, who said "I came that they might have life and have it more abundantly." This is a call to the Church in South Africa to help in the all-round development of Man in the present, and not only in the hereafter. In this regard, the people of South Africa, especially those who claim to be Christians, would be well advised to take heed of the Conference decisions of the World Council of Churches held at Cottesloe, Johannesburg, in 1960, which gave a clear lead on the mission of the Church in our day. It left no room for doubt about the relevancy of the Christian message in the present issues that confront mankind. I note with gratitude this broader outlook of the World Council of Churches. It has great meaning and significance for us in Africa.

There is nothing new in South Africa's apartheid ideas, but South Africa is unique in this: the ideas not only survive in our modern age, but are stubbornly defended, extended and bolstered up by legislation at the time, when in the major part of the world they are now largely historical and are either being shamefacedly hidden behind concealing formulations or are being steadily scrapped. These ideas survive in South Africa, because those who sponsor them profit from them.

They provide moral whitewash for the conditions, which exist in the country: for the fact that the country is ruled exclusively by a White government elected by an exclusively White electorate, which is a privileged minority; for the fact that 87 per cent of the land and all the best agricultural land within reach of town, market and railways is reserved for White ownership and occupation and now through the recent Group Areas legislation non-Whites are losing more land to White greed; for the fact that all skilled and highly-paid jobs are for Whites only; for the fact that all universities of any academic merit are an exclusive preserve of the Whites; for the fact that the education of every White child costs about £ 64 p.a., whilst that of an African child costs about £ 9 p.a. and that of an Indian child or Coloured child costs about £ 20 p.a.; for the fact that White education is universal and compulsory up to the age of 16, whilst education for the non-White children is scarce and inadequate, and for the fact that almost one million Africans a year are arrested and gaoled or fined for breaches of innumerable pass and permit laws, which do not apply to the Whites.

I could carry on in this strain, and talk on every facet of South African life from the cradle to the grave. But these facts today are becoming known to all the world. A fierce spotlight of world attention has been thrown on them. Try as our government and its apologists will, with honeyed words about "separate development" and "eventual independence" in so-called "Bantu homelands", nothing can conceal the reality of South African conditions. I, as a Christian, have always felt that there is one thing above all about "apartheid" or "separate development" that is unforgivable. It seems utterly indifferent to the suffering of individual persons, who lose their land, their homes, their jobs, in the pursuit of what is surely the most terrible dream in the world. This terrible dream is not held on to by a crackpot group on the fringe of society or by Ku-Klux Klansmen, of whom we have a sprinkling. It is the deliberate policy of a government, supported actively by a large part of the White population, and tolerated passively by an overwhelming White majority, but now fortunately rejected by an encouraging White minority, who have thrown their lot with the non-Whites, who are overwhelmingly opposed to so-called separate development.

Thus, it is that the golden age of Africa's independence is also the dark age of South Africa's decline and retrogression, brought about by men who, when revolutionary changes that entrenched fundamental human rights were taking place in Europe, were closed in at the tip of South Africa — and so missed the wind of progressive change.

In the wake of that decline and retrogression, bitterness between men grows to alarming heights; the economy declines as confidence ebbs away; unemployment rises; government becomes increasingly dictatorial and intolerant of constitutional and legal procedures, increasingly violent and suppressive; there is a constant drive for more policemen, more soldiers, more armaments, banishments without trial and penal whippings. All the trappings of medieval backwardness and cruelty come to the fore. Education is reduced to an instrument of subtle in-

29

doctrination, slanted and biased reporting in the organs of public information, a creeping censorship, book-banning and blacklisting — all these spread their shadows over the land. This is South Africa today, in the age of Africa's greatness.

But beneath the surface there is a spirit of defiance. The people of South Africa have never been a docile lot, least of all the African people. We have a long tradition of struggle for our national rights, reaching back to the very beginnings of White settlement and conquest 300 years ago.

Our history is one of opposition to domination, of protest and refusal to submit to tyranny. Consider some of our great names; the great warrior and nation-builder Chaka, who welded tribes into the Zulu nation from which I spring; Moshoeshoe, the statesman and nation-builder, who fathered the Basuto nation and placed Basutoland beyond the reach of the claws of the South African Whites; Hintsa of the Xhosas, who chose death rather than surrender his territory to the White invaders. All these and other royal names, as well as other great chieftains, resisted manfully White intrusion.

Consider also the sturdiness of the stock that nurtured the foregoing great names. I refer to our forbears, who in the trekking from the north to the southernmost tip of Africa centuries ago braved rivers that are perennially swollen; hacked their way through treacherous jungle and forest; survived the plagues of the then untamed lethal diseases of a multifarious nature that abounded in Equatorial Africa and wrested themselves from the gaping mouths of the beasts of prey. They endured it all. They settled in these parts of Africa to build a future worthwhile for us their offspring.

Whilst the social and political conditions have changed and the problems we face are different, we too, their progeny, find ourselves facing a situation, where we have to struggle for our very survival as human beings. Although the methods of struggle may differ from time to time, the universal human strivings for liberty remain unchanged. We in our situation have chosen the path of non-violence of our own volition. Along this path we have organised many heroic campaigns. All the strength of progressive leadership in South Africa, all my life and strength has

30

been given to the pursuance of this method, in an attempt to avert disaster in the interests of South Africa and have bravely paid the penalties for it.

It may well be that South Africa's social system is a monument to racialism and race oppression, but its people are a living testimony to the unconquerable spirit of mankind. Down the years, against seemingly overwhelming odds, they have sought the goal of fuller life and liberty, striving with incredible determination and fortitude for the right to live as men — as free men.

In this, our country is not unique. Your recent and inspiring history, when the Axis powers over-ran most European states, is testimony of this unconquerable spirit of mankind. People of Europe formed Resistance Movements that finally helped to break the power of the combination of Nazism and Fascism, with their creed of race arrogance and *herrenvolk* mentality.

Every people have, at one time or another in their history, been plunged into such struggle. But generally, the passing of time has seen the barriers to freedom going down, one by one. Not so in South Africa. Here the barriers do not go down. Each step we take forward, every achievement we chalk up, is cancelled out by the raising of new and higher barriers to our advance. The colour bars do not get weaker; they get stronger. The bitterness of the struggle mounts as liberty comes step by step closer to the freedom fighters' grasp. All too often, the protests and demonstrations of our people have been beaten back by force; but they have never been silenced.

Through all this cruel treatment in the name of law and order, our people, with a few exceptions, have remained non-violent. If today this peace Award is given to South Africa through a Black man, it is not because we in South Africa have won our fight for peace and human brotherhood. Far from it. Perhaps we stand farther from victory than any other people in Africa. But nothing which we have suffered at the hands of the government has turned us from our chosen path of disciplined resistance. It is for this, I believe, that this Award is given.

How easy it would have been in South Africa for the natural feelings of resentment at White domination to have been turned into feelings of hatred and a desire for revenge against the White community. Here, where every day in every aspect of life, every non-White comes up against the ubiquitous sign, "Europeans Only", and the equally ubiquitous policeman to enforce it — here it could well be expected that a racialism equal to that of their oppressors would flourish to counter the White arrogance towards Blacks. That it has not done so is no accident. It is because, deliberately and advisedly, African leadership for the past 50 years, with the inspiration of the African National Congress which I had the honour to lead for the last decade or so until it was banned, had set itself steadfastly against racial vaingloriousness.

We knew that in so doing we passed up opportunities for easy demagogic appeal to the natural passions of a people denied freedom and liberty; we discarded the chance of an easy and expedient emotional appeal. Our vision has always been that of a non-racial democratic South Africa which upholds the rights of all who live in our country, to remain there as full citizens with equal rights and responsibilities with all others. For the consumation of this ideal we have laboured unflinchingly. We shall continue to labour unflinchingly.

It is this vision, which prompted the African National Congress to invite members of other racial groups, who believe with us in the brotherhood of man and in the freedom of all people to join with us in establishing a non-racial democratic South Africa. Thus, the African National Congress in its day brought about the Congress Alliance and welcomed the emergence of the Liberal Party and the Progressive Party, who to an encouraging measure support these ideals.

The true patriots of South Africa, for whom I speak, will be satisfied with nothing less than the fullest democratic rights. In government we will not be satisfied with anything less than direct individual adult suffrage and the right to stand for and be elected to all organs of the government. In economic matters, we will be satisfied with nothing less than equality of opportunity in every sphere and the enjoyment by all of those heritages, which form the resources of the country, which up to now have been appropriated on a racial "Whites Only" basis. In culture, we will be satisfied with nothing less than the opening of all doors of learning to non-segregatary institutions on the sole criterion of ability. In the social sphere we will be satisfied with nothing less than the abolition of all racial bars.

We do not demand these things for peoples of African descent alone. We demand them for all South Africans, White and Black. On these principles we are uncompromising. To compromise would be an expediency that is most treacherous to democracy, for in the turn of events the sweets of economic, political and social privileges that are a monopoly of only one section of a community turn sour even in the mouths of those who eat them. Thus, apartheid in practice is proving to be a monster created by Frankenstein. That is the tragedy of the South African scene.

Many spurious slogans have been invented in our country in an effort to redeem uneasy race relations—"trusteeship", "separate development", "race federation" and elsewhere "partnership." These are efforts to sidetrack us from the democratic road, mean delaying tactics that fool no one but the unwary. No euphemistic naming will ever hide their hideous nature. We reject these policies because they do great offence to man's sublime aspirations that have remained true in a sea of flux and change down the ages, aspirations of which the United Nations Declaration of Human Rights is a culmination. This is what we stand for. This is what we fight for.

In their fight for lasting values, there are many things that have sustained the spirit of the freedom-loving people of South Africa and those in the yet unredeemed parts of Africa, where the White man claims resolutely propriety rights over democracy — a universal heritage. High amongst them — the things that have sustained us, stand the magnificent support of the progressive people and governments throughout the world, amongst whom number the people and government of the country of which I am today a guest; our brothers in Africa; especially in the independent African States, organisations who share the outlook we embrace in countries scattered right across the face of the globe; the United Nations Organisation jointly and some of its member-nations singly. In their defence of peace in the world through actively upholding the quality of

33

man, all these groups have reinforced our undying faith in the unassailable rightness and justness of our cause. To all of them I say:

> Alone we would have been weak. Our heartfelt appreciation of your acts of support to us. We cannot adequately express, nor can we ever forget, now or in the future when victory is behind us. And, South Africa's freedom rests in the hands of all her people.

We, South Africans, however, equally understand that much as others might do for us, our freedom cannot come to us as a gift from abroad. Our freedom we must make ourselves. All honest freedom-loving people have dedicated themselves to that task. What we need is the courage that rises with danger.

Whatever may be the future of our freedom efforts, our cause is the cause of the liberation of people, who are denied freedom. Only on this basis can the peace of Africa and the world be firmly founded. Our cause is the cause of equality between nations and peoples. Only thus can the brotherhood of man be firmly established. It is encouraging and elating to remind you that despite her humiliation and torment at the hands of White rule, the spirit of Africa in quest of freedom has been, generally, for peaceful means to the utmost.

If I have dwelt at length on my country's race problem, it is not as though other countries on our continent do not labour under these problems, but because it is here in the Republic of South Africa that the race problem is most acute. Perhaps, in no other country on the continent is White supremacy asserted with greater vigour and determination and a sense of righteousness. This places the opponents of apartheid in the front rank of those who fight White domination.

In bringing my address to a close, let me invite Africa to cast her eyes beyond the past and to some extent the present, with its woes and tribulations, trials and failures, and some successes, and see herself as an emerging continent, bursting to freedom through the shell of centuries of serfdom. This is Africa's age — the dawn of her fulfilment, yes, the moment, when she must grapple with destiny to reach the summits of sublimity

34

saying — ours was a fight for noble values and worthy ends, and not for lands and the enslavement of man.

Africa is a vital subject matter in the world of today, a focal point of world interest and concern. Could it not be that history has delayed her rebirth for a purpose? The situation confronts her with inescapable challenges, but more importantly with opportunities for service to herself and mankind. She evades the challenges and neglects the opportunities to her shame, if not her doom. How she sees her destiny is a more vital and rewarding quest than bemoaning her past with its humiliations and sufferings. The address could do no more than pose some questions and leave it to the African leaders and peoples to provide satisfying answers and responses by their concern for higher values and by their noble actions that could be:

"...footprints on the sands of time.

"Footprints, that perhaps another,
Sailing o'er life's solemn main,
A forlorn and shipwrecked brother,
Seeing, shall take heart again."

Still licking, the scars of past wrongs perpetrated on her, could she not be magnanimous and practise no revenge? Her hand of friendship scornfully rejected, her pleas for justice and fairplay spurned, should she not nonetheless seek to turn enmity into amity?

Though robbed of her lands, her independence and opportunities — this, oddly enough, often in the name of civilisation and even Christianity, should she not see her destiny as being that of making a distinctive contribution to human progress and human relationship, with a peculiar new African flavour enriched by the diversity of cultures she enjoys, thus building on the summits of present human achievement on edifice that would be one of the finest tributes to the genius of man? She should see this hour of her fulfilment as a challenge to labour on until she is purged of racial domination, and as an opportunity of reassuring the world that her national aspiration lies, not in overthrowing White domination to replace it by a Black caste, but in building a non-racial democracy

35

that shall be a monumental brotherhood, a "brotherly community" with none discriminated against on grounds of race of colour.

What of the many pressing and complex political, economic and cultural problems attendant upon the early years of a newly-independent State? These, and others which are the legacy of colonial days, will tax to the limit the statesmanship, ingenuity, altruism and steadfastness of African leadership and its unbending avowal to democratic tenets in statecraft. To us all, free or not free, the call of the hour is to redeem the name and honour of Mother Africa. In a strife-torn world, tottering on the brink of complete destruction by man-made nuclear weapons, a free and independent Africa is in the making, in answer to the injunction and challenge of history: "Arise and shine, for thy light is come."

Acting in concert with other nations, she is man's last hope for a mediator between the East and West and is qualified to demand of the great powers to "turn the swords into ploughshares" because two-thirds of mankind is hungry and illiterate; to engage human energy, human skill and human talent in the service of peace, for the alternative is unthinkable — war, destruction and desolation; and to build a world community, which will stand as a lasting monument to the millions of men and women, to such devoted and distinguished world citizens and fighters for peace as the late Dag Hammarskjold, who have given their lives that we may live in happiness and peace. Africa's qualification for this noble task is incontestable, for her own fight has never been and is not now a fight for conquest of land, for accumulation of wealth or domination of peoples, but for the recognition and preservation of the rights of man and the establishment of a truly free world for a free people.

OLIVER TAMBO ON NELSON MANDELA

(Here is the "introduction" by Oliver Tambo to Nelson Mandela's celebrated book, *No Easy Walk To Freedom*: *Articles, Speeches and Trial Addresses* published by Heinemann, London (1965). It was edited by (the late) Ruth First and it carried a foreword by Ahmed Ben Bella, then President of Algeria.)

MANDELA AND TAMBO said the brass plate on our office door. We practised as attorneys·at-law in Johannesburg in a shabby building across the street from the Magistrates' Court. Chancellor House in Fox Street was one of the few buildings in which African tenants could hire offices: it was owned by Indians. This was before the axe of the Group Areas Act fell to declare the area "White" and landlords were themselves prosecuted if they did not evict the Africans. MANDELA AND TAMBO was written huge across the frosted window panes on the second floor, and the letters stood out like a challenge. To White South Africa it was bad enough that two men with Black skins should practise as lawyers, but it was indescribably worse that the letters also spelled out our political partnership.

Nelson and I were both born in the Transkei, he one year after me. We were students together at Fort Hare University College. With others we had founded the African National Congress Youth League. We went together into the Defiance Campaign of 1952, into general strikes against the government and sat in the same Treason Trial dock.

For years we worked side by side in the offices near the Courts. To reach our desks each morning, Nelson and I ran the gauntlet of patient queues of people overflowing from the chairs in the waiting-room into the corridors. South Africa has the dubious reputation of boasting one of the highest prison populations in the world. Jails are jam-packed with Africans imprisoned for serious offences—and crimes of violence are ever on the increase in apartheid society—but also for petty infringements of statutory law that no really civilized society would punish with imprisonment. To be unemployed is a crime because no African can for long evade arrest if his passbook does not carry the stamp of authorized and approved employment. To be landless can be a crime, and we interviewed weekly the delegations of grizzled, weather-worn peasants from the countryside, who came to tell us how many generations of their families had worked a little piece of land from which they were now being ejected. To brew African beer, to drink it or to use the proceeds to supplement the meagre family income is a crime, and women who do so face heavy fines and jail terms. To cheek a White man can be a crime. To live in the "wrong" area—an area declared White or Indian or Coloured—can be a crime for Africans. South African apartheid laws turn innumerable innocent people into "criminals." Apartheid stirs hatred and frustration among people. Young people, who should be in school or learning a trade, roam the streets, join gangs and wreak their revenge on the society that confronts them with only the dead-end alley of crime or poverty.

Our buff office files carried thousands of these stories and if, when we started our law partnership, we had not been rebels against South African apartheid, our experiences in our offices would have remedied the deficiency. We had risen to professional status in our community, but every case in court, every visit to the prisons to interview clients, reminded us of the humiliation and suffering burning into our people.

Nelson, one of the royal family of the Transkei, was groomed from childhood for respectability, status and sheltered living. Born near Umtata in 1918, he was the eldest son of a Tembu chief. His father died when he was 12 and his upbringing and education were taken over by the Paramount Chief. Nelson, Sabata, Paramount Chief of the Tembu and opponent of the

Government and Kaizer Matanzima, Chief Minister of the Transkei and arch-collaborator with the Nationalist Government, were educated together. At the age of 16, Nelson went to Fort Hare and there we first met: in the thick of a student strike.

After Fort Hare, we parted company. I went on to teach mathematics as St. Peter's School in Johannesburg. From this school, killed by the government in later years because it refused to bow its head to government-dictated principles of a special education for "inferior" Africans (Bantu education), graduated successive series of young men drawn inexorably into the African National Congress, because it was the head of our patriotic, national movement for our rights.

Nelson ran away from the Transkei to escape a tribal marriage his cousins and uncles were trying to arrange for him. In Johannesburg, he had his first encounter with the lot of the urban African in a teeming African township: overcrowding, incessant raids for passes, arrests, poverty, the pin-pricks and frustrations of the White rule. Walter Sisulu, Secretary-General of the African National Congress in a vital period, befriended and advised and urged him to study law. Mandela studied by correspondence to gain an arts degree, enrolled for a law degree at the University of the Witwatersrand and was later articled to a firm of White attorneys. We met again in 1944 in the ranks of the African National Congress Youth League.

As a man, Nelson is passionate, emotional, sensitive, quickly stung to bitterness and retaliation by insult and patronage. He has a natural air of authority. He cannot help magnetizing a crowd: he is commanding with a tall, handsome bearing; trusts and is trusted by the youth, for their impatience reflects his own; appealing to the women. He is dedicated and fearless. He is the born mass leader.

But early on, he came to understand that State repression was too savage to permit mass meetings and demonstrations through which the people could ventilate their grievances and hope for redress. It was of limited usefulness to head great rallies. The government did not listen and soon enough the tear gas and the muzzles of the guns were turned against the people. The justice of our cries went unrecognized. The popularity of leaders like Mandela was an invitation to counter-attack by the government. Mandela was banned from speaking, from attending gatherings, from leaving Johannesburg, from belonging to any organization. Speeches, demonstrations, peaceful protests, political organizing became illegal.

Of all that group of young men, Mandela and his close friend and co-leader, Walter Sisulu, were perhaps the fastest to get to grips with the harsh realities of the African struggle against the most powerful adversary in Africa: a highly industrialized, well-armed state, manned by a fanatical group of White men determined to defend their privilege and their prejudice, and aided by the complicity of American, British, West German, and Japanese investment in the most profitable system of oppression on the continent. Nelson was a key figure in thinking, planning and devising new tactics.

We had to forge an alliance of strength based not on colour but on commitment to the total abolition of apartheid and oppression; we would seek allies, of whatever colour, as long as they were totally agreed on our liberation aims. The African people, by nature of their numbers, their militancy, and the grimness of their oppression, would be the spearhead of the struggle. We had to organize the people, in town and countryside, as an instrument for struggle. Mandela drafted the "M" plan, a simple commonsense plan for organization on a street basis, so that Congress volunteers would be in daily touch with the people, alert to their needs and able to mobilize them. He no longer appeared on the public platform and few platforms were allowed us as the years went by, but he was ever among the people, guiding his lieutenants to organize them. During the Treason Trial these efforts at organization were put on trial. Mandela went from prison cell to dock and then to witness-box, when the accused conducted their defence and he and his co-accused expounded the policy of Congress in court. The men in the dock were acquitted, but the trial marked the end of that epoch and the opening of a new one.

By 1960, virtually every African leader was muzzled and restrict-

40

ed by government decree. There was no right to organize. In March, 1960, there were the anti-pass protests called by the breakaway Pan-Africanist Congress, and the peaceful gathering at Sharpeville was machine-gunned. The ANC called for a national protest strike.

The country answered that call. The ANC was declared illegal, together with the Pan-Africanist Congress. In a five-month-long State of Emergency, virtually every known Congressman was imprisoned, but during the Emergency and even more so immediately afterwards the ANC put itself on an underground footing. Now Mandela's "M" plan came into its own. Ever at the centre, pulling the strings together, inspiring the activities that, if apprehended, could mean long stretches in prison for ANC activists, was Nelson.

In May, 1961, South Africa was to be declared a Nationalist Republic. There was a White referendum, but no African was consulted. The African people decided there were ways of making their opposition felt. A general strike would be the answer. The strike was called in the name of Nelson Mandela. He left his home, our office, his wife and children, to live the life of a political outlaw. Here began the legend of the "Black Pimpernel." He lived in hiding, meeting only his closest political associates, travelling round the country in disguise, popping up here to lead and advise, disappearing again when the hunt got too hot.

The strike was smashed by an unprecedented police and army mobilization. If peaceful protests like these were to be put down by force then the people would be forced to use other methods of struggle; this was the inevitable conclusion. The ANC was no longer merely a national patriotic front, it was an underground resistance struggle. Acts of sabotage shook the country from the second half of 1961. "Umkhonto we Sizwe" (the Spear of the Nation) had been formed and was at work.

I had left South Africa early in 1960, sent out by the ANC to open our office abroad. Mandela was then in prison during the State of Emergency proclaimed after Sharpeville. I saw him again, astonishingly, in 1961 and 1962, when he left his hiding places somewhere in South Africa, was smuggled across the border and turned up at the Addis Ababa conference of the Pan-African Freedom Movement of East and Central Africa to expound before the delegates the policy for the struggle of our organization and our people.

In South Africa, the freedom fight has grown grim and relentless. Mandela went home to survive a perilous existence underground for 17 months until he was betrayed by an informer and sentenced to five years' imprisonment for his leadership of the 1961 strike and for leaving the country illegally. From his cell, he was taken to the dock in the Rivonia Trial to face trial with eight others—among them Walter Sisulu. The charge was sabotage and conspiracy to overthrow the government by force. The world watched that trial and knows the verdict of guilty and the sentence of life imprisonment. Nelson Mandela is in Robben Island today. His inspiration lives on in the heart of every African patriot. He is the symbol of the self-sacrificing leadership our struggle has thrown up and our people need. He is unrelenting, yet capable of flexibility and delicate judgement. He is an outstanding individual, but he knows that he derives his strength from the great masses of people, who make up the freedom struggle in our country.

I am convinced that the world-wide protests during the Rivonia Trial saved Mandela and his fellow-accused from the death sentence. But in South Africa, a life sentence means imprisonment until death — or until the defeat of the government, which holds these men prisoners. The sentences they serve are a scaring reminder that such men must not be wasted behind bars; that no solution to South Africa's conflict can be found, while the people are deprived of such leadership; that Mandela is imprisoned not for his personal defiance of apartheid law but because he asserted the claims of a whole people living and dying under the most brutal system of race rule the world knows.

A Postscript: *Nelson Mandela on Oliver Tambo*: "Oliver Tambo is much more than a brother to me. He is my greatest friend and comrade for nearly 50 years." — NELSON MANDELA (In a message from the prison, February, 1985)

42

TAMBO ON MANDELA AND
THE NEHRU AWARD

When the 1979 Jawaharlal Nehru Award for International Understanding was announced, there was jubiliation and dismay as the awardee was Nelson Rolihlahla Mandela— the outstanding South African leader behind bars in the high security Robben Island prison of South Africa. However, in 1980, at the award presentation ceremony in Delhi, Oliver Tambo deputised for his friend, law partner and fellow freedom-fighter, Mandela. Here below is the statement made by Tambo on that occasion after receiving the award on behalf of Mandela.

Today, as Nelson Rolihlahla Mandela moves around the restricted confines of his prison cell on Robben Island, his mind is tuned in to the proceedings in Delhi. He shares this pre-occupation not only with his beloved wife, Winnie Mandela, herself the subject of heartless restrictions and bans, but also with Walter Sisulu, Ahmed Kathrada, James April, Toivo Ya Toivo and other national leaders and fighters for liberation, for democracy and justice—fellow inmates of the notorious Robben Island prison. The thoughts of the entire membership of the ANC and of its allies and friends converge today on Delhi. The vast majority of the people of South Africa, from all walks of life and all strata and race origins — the young, no less than the old, regard this day in New Delhi as a national occasion for them.

It is, therefore, my pleasant duty, on behalf of the National Executive Committee of the African National Congress, to express the deep appreciation and gratitude of all the national leaders and patriots incarcerated in the prisons of apartheid, all the members, allies and friends of the ANC and the great masses of the people engaged in the liberation struggle of our country, for the great honour bestowed on Nelson Mandela in nominating him for the 1979 Jawaharlal Nehru Award for International Understanding.

It is equally and especially my pleasant duty, although a much more onerous one, to convey to Your Excellency, Mr President, to the Prime Minister and to your Government and people, the heartfelt thanks of our colleague, brother and comrade, Nelson Mandela.

He received the news of the Jawaharlal Nehru Award with a mixture of disbelief, surprise, profound gratitude and excitement. But the excitement quickly mellowed into a deep sense of humility. For, he understands the full meaning of the Award, its enormous significance and its challenging implications for him and his people.

He understands, because he knows Pandit Nehru's imposing stature as a world statesman; he knows his revered place in the hearts, minds and lives of the 650 million people of India; he knows, too, the esteem and deep respect Pandit Nehru enjoyed among the peoples of Asia, Africa and Latin America.

Nelson Mandela, therefore, accepts the Award with full awareness of its historic message. He accepts it as a supreme challenge to him personally and to the leadership of the ANC and the people of South Africa of all races. He accepts it as an honour less for him than for the people of Africa.

We, of the African National Congress, wish to pay special tribute to the penetrating vision of the Jury of the Jawaharlal Nehru Award for International Understanding: The recipient, Nelson Mandela, is beyond the reach of society. For more than 18 years, he has travelled and appeared nowhere, his voice has remained unheard and his views unexpressed. In that time, momentous world events have occurred sufficient to put into complete oblivion any one not involved in the main current of developments. We mention a few of these developments, limiting ourselves to Africa only.

A long-cherished dream of the ANC came true with the formation of the OAU in 1963. The continent has torn asunder almost every chain of colonial bondage and joined the world community of nations as a full and equal member, contributing with great effect to the solution of international problems. Southern Africa has undergone geo-political transformations and social upheavals in the course of which colonial foundations, some of them laid 500 years ago, have been reduced to a heap of ruins. New names have appeared on the international scene and now stand out as great landmarks defining the geo-political landscape of Southern Africa: Samora Machel, Kenneth Kaunda, Agostinho Neto, Seretse Khama, Julius Nyerere, Joshua Nkomo, Robert Mugabe and Sam Nujoma. The South African Defence Force, mighty in its arms and proud of its record, has had the traumatic experience of being defeated for the first time in its history by the armed forces of a newly independent state, and barely three months later, the same army was unleashing its might upon small children who confronted its bullets with only dustbin-lids and stones in Soweto. South Africa has suffered the staggering "Information Scandal," which climaxed in the fall of Vorster and Van den Bergh, of whom it could be said: No two South Africans have been more faithful to Hitler and his ways and none more identified with the naked inhumanity of the apartheid system.

Their place has been taken by P.W. Botha and Piet Koornhof, who, fighting no less relentlessly for the permanence of White minority rule in South Africa, have given fresh impetus to the dynamics of revolutionary change by their remarkable and disastrous failure to distinguish between the forgotten era of J.C. Smuts and Jan Hofmeyr — when the African giant was still lying prostrate, in chains — and the present hour, when the people's demand for power enjoys universal support and can no longer be compromised.

For, the question in South Africa today is no longer what amendments should be made to the law, but who makes the law and the amendments. Is it the people of South Africa as a whole or a White minority group with not even a democratic mandate from the majority of the people? An organ like the so-called Presidential Council is wholly objectionable not because Africans are excluded from it, but because it is a studied insult to the Black people. It represents a policy decision for, and not by, the majority of South Africans. If this is the practice today, it was the practice in 1910 and since. But today, the people of South Africa are challenging the very constitutional foundations of the Republic of South Africa. Hence, the struggle for the seizure of power.

The stormy succession of tumultuous events of the kind we have mentioned were sufficient to drive Nelson Mandela and his Robben Island colleagues out of our minds. Yet, he and the other jailed national leaders have a presence in the consciousness of our people and of the world public so powerful that it cannot be explained except in terms of the indestructibility of the cause to which they have surrendered their liberty and offered their lives — the cause of the oppressed majority in South Africa, the cause of Africa, the cause of progressive mankind.

The unique significance of the 1979 Jawaharlal Nehru Award is that, displaying a delicate sensitivity to this enduring presence, it has identified in Nelson Mandela the indomitable spirit of a people, the supreme justice of their cause and their resolute determination to win final victory. In our humble opinion, the Jury of the Jawaharlal Nehru Award for International Understanding could have made no better choice among the people of South Africa for such an honour at this time. For, if the immediate reaction of racist Prime Minister P.W. Botha to the victory of the Patriotic Front Alliance in Zimbabwe was to invite the people of South Africa to a multi-racial conference to discuss the future of that country, the oppressed millions, supported by White democrats, responded by demanding the release of Nelson Mandela from imprisonment. The fact that P.M. Botha was evidently only trying to diffuse an explosive situation in South Africa subtracts nothing from the centrality of Nelson Mandela's past, present and future role in the struggle to unite the people of South Africa as fellow citizens in a democratic, non-racial and peaceful country. His entire political life has been guided by the vision of a democratic South Africa, its people united across the barriers of race,

46

colour and religion, and contributing as a single nation to the pursuit of international peace and progress. For this reason, he knows no distinction between the struggle and his life.

Having chosen the law, as the avenue through which he could best serve his people, he soon found that the legal system of apartheid was itself an instrument of oppression. His conscience dictated that he place the quest for justice above the administration of unjust laws. This concern for justice led him into politics, into the leadership of the African National Congress, and ultimately to Robben Island—and even more politics.

It is opportune to recall, and Nelson Mandela's captors may wish to ponder the fact that Jawaharlal Nehru, who was no stranger to imprisonment and was in no way destroyed by it, served the world community, including the British, far better as a free man than as a political prisoner. Nelson Mandela's 18 years' imprisonment has in no way destroyed him, and will not. Indeed a striking feature of political imprisonment in South Africa is that the morale of the prisoners remains intact notwithstanding the harsh brutality of the prison conditions and the long duration of the prison sentences.

The demand for the release of Nelson Mandela and all political prisoners is world-wide and is made more in the interests of all South Africans than out of any sense of unwanted pity for those imprisoned. But, overwhelmed by their iniquitous past and present, and lacking in true courage, the self-appointed rulers of our country fear the future: they are frightened of democracy, scared of social progress and suspicious of peace. That is why Nelson Mandela and some of the best known of our leaders remain in prison.

That is why it seems inevitable that the road to our liberation will be vastly different from yours Mr. President. When India celebrated 25 years of independence, you observed, in your publication, "India 1973," that "twenty-five years ago ... the British transferred power to the rightful rulers of the country, the people of India. The event was unique for at least one reason: the transfer of power was effected not as a consequence of a clash of arms, but as the culmination of a non-violent revolution led by Mahatma Gandhi, the greatest apostle of peace and non-violence in modern times."

The revolution in South Africa has already lost its non-violent character. Twenty-five years ago this year, in the course of a powerful non-violent struggle led by one of the greatest leaders in South African history, Chief A.J. Lutuli, late President-General of the ANC and winner of the Nobel Peace Prize for 1960, the people of South Africa adopted the Freedom Charter -- a blueprint for democracy, progress and peace, which has itself gained international recognition as the key to a happy and peaceful future for South Africa.

But a mere six years after the adoption of the Freedom Charter, the oppressed people of South Africa were compelled to choose between violence and cowardice, to decide whether to fight or to surrender. They rejected cowardice. They refused to surrender. They took up arms. Africa and the world community approved and endorsed their decision.

Unlike India, therefore, South Africa holds out no conceivable prospect for a peaceful transfer of power to the people of South Africa. And yet, there is a golden thread that has linked the people of India and South Africa over the centuries.

Jan van Riebeeck, of the Dutch East India Company, was on a voyage to the seaports of India and the Far East when, in 1652, he stopped in South Africa, and there planted a problem, which the United Nations has been debating since its foundation, and which the UN General Assembly is discussing this very week.

It is fitting that on this day, I should recall the long and glorious struggle of those *South Africans*, who came to our shores from India 120 years ago. Within two years of entering the bondage of indentured labour, Indian workers staged their first strike against the working conditions in Natal. This was possibly the first general strike in South African history. Their descendants, working and fighting for the future of their country, South Africa, have retained the tradition of militant struggle and are today an integral part of the mass-based liberation movement in South Africa.

But the striking role of India in the development of the struggle

48

for national and social liberation in South Africa has its firm roots in the early campaigns led by Mahatma Gandhi in that country, coupled with the continuing and active interest he took in the South African situation. All South Africans have particular cause to honour and remember the man, who was in our midst for 21 years and went on to enter the history books as the Father of Free India. His imprint on the course of the South African struggle is indelible.

In the 1970's, in South Africa and India, our people voiced the same sentiments; to wage a war in the name of freedom and democracy, they said, was a hollow mockery as long as the colonial peoples were not free. We applauded the "Quit India" demand against the British, for, as the Congress resolution in August, 1942, so correctly said: "India...the classic land of modern imperialism, has become the crux of the question, for by the freedom of India will Britain and the United Nations be judged, and the peoples of Asia and Africa be filled with hope and enthusiasm." And so we were filled with hope and enthusiasm as we watched events unfold in India.

If Mahatma Gandhi started and fought his heroic struggle in South Africa and India, Jawaharlal Nehru was to continue it in Asia, Africa and internationally. In 1946, India broke trade relations with South Africa — the first country to do so. In the same year, at the first Session of the UN General Assembly, the Indian Government sharply raised the question of racial discrimination in South Africa — again the first country to take this action.

Speaking at the Bandung Conference in April 1955, Jawaharlal Nehru declared: "There is nothing more terrible than the infinite tragedy of Africa in the past few hundred years."

Referring to "the days when millions of Africans were carried away as galley slaves to America and elsewhere, half of them dying in the galleys." he urged: "we must accept responsibility for it, all of us, even though we ourselves were not directly involved."

He continued... "But unfortunately, in a different sense, even now the tragedy of Africa is greater than that of any other

49

continent, whether it is racial or political. It is up to Asia to help Africa to the best of her ability because we are sister continents."

To her great honour, India has consistently lived upto this historic declaration, which constitutes one of the cornerstones of the Non-Aligned Movement. The tragedy of Africa, in racial and political terms, is now concentrated in the Southern tip of the continent — in South Africa, Namibia, and in a special sense, Robben Island.

Quite clearly we have all come a long way from 1955. Jawaharlal Nehru's clarion call has already translated itself into a lasting partnership of the peoples of Asia, Africa and Latin-America, who have joined hands with the Socialist community of nations, the progressive forces of the world and the national liberation movement, in an anti-imperialist front to eradicate the last vestiges of colonial domination and racism in Africa and elsewhere, to end fascism and exploitation, and to promote a new world economic order that will ensure true democracy, social progress and peace.

Nelson Mandela, who gained political maturity in the company of such household names in South Africa as A.J. Lutuli, Moses Kotane, Yusuf Dadoo, J.B. Marks, Elias Moretsele, Z.K. Matthews, Monty Naicker, Walter Sisulu, Lillian Ngoyi, Bram Fischer, Govan Mbeki, Helen Joseph and many others, has been confirmed by the Jawaharlal Nehru Award as a leader of men, ranking among the great international leaders of modern times. In their struggle for the seizure of power, the people of South Africa — its youth, workers, women, intelligentsia and peasants, led by the African National Congress and its allies, will not betray this great honour to our country. Nelson Mandela, with the rest of the leadership of the ANC, will remain worthy of the great Jawaharlal Nehru, today, tomorrow, ever.

The struggle to rid South Africa of racism, apartheid and colonial domination continues and victory for the world anti-imperialist forces is certain.

MANDELA'S LETTER TO INDIA STOPPED BY PRISON OFFICIALS

Nelson Mandela was chosen as the recipient of India's prestigious Jawaharlal Nehru Award for International Understanding for 1979.

In that connection, he wrote a letter from the Robben Island prison on August 3, 1980, to (Mrs) Manorama Bhalla, Secretary of the Indian Council for Cultural Relations, New Delhi, which administers the award. The letter was held up by prison authorities. It was smuggled out of prison and later circulated by the Indian Council for Cultural Relations, a year later on August 26, 1981. This letter is reproduced here.

The South African regime refused permission for (Mrs) Winnie Mandela to receive the award on behalf of her husband. It was received in November, 1980, by Oliver Tambo, President of the African National Congress on behalf of Mandela at an impressive ceremony in New Delhi.

Dear Mrs. Bhalla,

I am writing to express my sincere thanks and appreciation to the Indian Council for Cultural Relations for honouring me with the 1979 "Jawaharlal Nehru Award for International Understanding." Although I have been singled out for this award, I am mindful that I am the mere medium for an honour that rightly belongs to the people of our country.

Our people cannot but feel humble, at the same time proud that one of their number has been selected to join the distinguished men and women who have been similarly honoured in the past.

51

I recall these names because to my mind they symbolize not only the scope and nature of the award, but they in turn constitute a fitting tribute to the great man after whom it has been named—Pandit Jawaharlal Nehru. The lives and varied contribution of each one of them reflect in some measure, the rich and many-sided life of Panditji: selfless humanitarian Mother Teresa, international statesman Josip Broz Tito, notable political leaders, Julius Nyerere and Kenneth Kaunda, medical benefactor, Jonas Salk and civil rights leader, Martin Luther King.

Truly Jawaharlal Nehru was an outstanding man. A combination of many men into one: freedom fighter, politician, world statesman, prison graduate, master of the English language, lawyer and historian. As one of the pioneers of the Non-Aligned Movement, he has made a lasting contribution to world peace and the brotherhood of man.

In the upsurge of anti-colonial and freedom struggles that swept through Asia and Africa in the post-war period there could hardly be a liberation movement or national leader, who was not influenced in one way or another by the thoughts, activities and example of Pandit Nehru and the All India Congress (Indian National Congress—Editor). If I may presume to look back on my own political education and upbringing, I find that my own ideas were influenced by his experience.

While at university and engrossed in student politics, I, for the first time, became familiar with the name of this famous man. In the 'forties, for the first time I read one of his books, *The Unity of India*. It made an indelible impression on my mind and ever since then, I procured, read and treasured any one of his works that became available.

When reading his autobiography or *Glimpses of World History*, one is left with the overwhelming impact of the immense scope of his ideas and breadth of his vision. Even in prison, he refused to succumb to a disproportionate concern with mundane matters or the material hardships of his environment. Instead, he devoted himself to creative activity and produced writings which will remain a legacy to generations of freedom lovers.

"Walls are dangerous companions", he wrote, "they may occasionally protect from outside evil and keep out an unwelcome intruder. But they also make you a prisoner and a slave, and you purchase your so-called purity and immunity at the cost of freedom. And the most terrible of walls are the walls that grow up in the mind, which prevent you from discarding an evil tradition simply because it is old, and from accepting a new thought because it is novel."

Like most young men in circumstances similar to ours, the politically inclined youth of my generation too were drawn together by feelings of an intense, but narrow form of nationalism. However, with experience, coupled with the unfurling of events at home and abroad, we acquired new perspectives and, as the horizon broadened, we began to appreciate the inadequacy of some youthful ideas. Time was to teach us, as Panditji says, that:

"...nationalism is good in its place, but is an unreliable friend and an unsafe historian. It blinds us to many happenings and sometimes distorts the truth, especially when it concerns us and our country ..."

In a world in which breathtaking advances in technology and communication have shortened the space between the erstwhile prohibitively distant lands; where outdated beliefs and imaginary differences among the people were being rapidly eradicated, where exclusiveness was giving way to cooperation and interdependence, we too found ourselves obliged to shed our narrow outlook and adjust to fresh realities.

Like the All-India Congress, one of the premier national liberation movements of the colonial world, we too began to assess our situation in a global context. We quickly learned the admonition of a great political thinker and teacher that no people in one part of the world could really be free while their brothers in other parts were still under foreign rule.

Our people admired the solidarity the All-India Congress displayed with the people of Ethiopia whose country was being ravaged by Fascist Italy. We observed that undeterred by labels, the All-India Congress courageously expressed its sympathy with Republican Spain. We were inspired when we learned of

53

the Congress Medical Mission to China in 1938. We noted that while the imperialist powers were hoping and even actively conniving to thrust the barbarous forces of Nazism against the Soviet Union, Panditji publicly spurned a pressing invitation to visit Mussolini, and two years later he again refused an invitation to Nazi Germany. Instead, he chose to go to Czechoslovakia, a country betrayed and dismembered by the infamous Munich deal.

In noting the internationalism of the All-India Congress and its leadership, we recalled the profound explanation of Mahatma Gandhi, when he said:

> "There is no limit to extending our service to our neighbours across state-made frontiers. God never made these frontiers."

It would be a grave omission on our part if we failed to mention the close bonds that have existed between our people and the people of India, and to acknowledge the encouragement, the inspiration and the practical assistance we have received as a result of the international outlook of the All-India Congress.

The oldest existing political organization in South Africa, the Natal Indian Congress, was founded by Mahatma Gandhi in 1894. He became its first secretary and in 21 years of his stay in South Africa, we were to witness the birth of ideas and methods of struggle that have exerted an incalculable influence on the history of the peoples of India and South Africa. Indeed it was on South African soil that Mahatmaji founded and embraced the philosophy of Satyagraha.

After his return to India, Mahatmaji's South African endeavours were to become the cause of the All-India Congress and the people of India as a whole. On the eve of India's independence Pandit Nehru said:

> "Long years ago, we made a tryst with destiny and now the time comes when we should redeem our pledge ... At the stroke of the midnight hour when the world sleeps India will awaken to life and freedom. ... It is fitting that at this solemn moment we take a pledge of dedication to the service

of India and her people and to the still larger cause of humanity."

Our people did not have to wait long to witness how uppermost our cause was in Panditji's mind when he made this pledge. The determination with which his gifted sister, Mrs. Vijayalakshmi Pandit as free India's Ambassador to the United Nations, won universal solidarity with our plight, and made her the beloved spokesman of the voiceless masses not only of our country and Namibia but of people like ours throughout the world. We were gratified to see that the pronouncements and efforts of the Congress during the independence struggle were now being actively pursued as the policy of the Government of India.

At the Asian People's Conference in Bombay in 1947, at Bandung in 1955, at the Commonwealth deliberations, in the Non-Aligned Movement, everywhere and at all times, Panditji and free India espoused our cause consistently.

Today, we are deeply inspired to witness his equally illustrious daughter Mrs. Indira Gandhi, continue along the same path with undiminished vitality and determination. Her activities, her interest, her pronouncements, remain for us a constant source of hope and encouragement.

India's championing of our cause assumes all the more significance, when we consider that ours is but one of the 153 countries, which constitute the family of nations and our over 21 million people, a mere fraction of the world's population. Moreover, our hardships, though great, become small in the context of a turbulent world enveloped by conflict, wars, famine, malnutrition, disease, poverty, illiteracy and hatred.

However, it is precisely India's exemplary role in world affairs that also serves to remind us that our problems, acute as they are, are part of humanity's problems and no part of the world can dare consider itself free of them unless and until the day the last vestige of man-made suffering is eradicated from every corner of the world.

This knowledge of shared suffering, though formidable in dimension, at the same time keeps alive in us our oneness with mankind and our own global responsibilities that accrue there-from. It also helps to strengthen our faith and belief in our future. To invoke once more the words of Panditji:

"In a world which is full of conflict and hatred and violence, it becomes more necessary than at any other time to have faith in human destiny. If the future we work for is full of hope for humanity, then the ills of the present do not matter much and we have justification for working for that future."

In this knowledge we forge ahead firm in our beliefs, strengthened by the devotion and solidarity of our friends; above all by an underlying faith in our own resources and determination and in the invincibility of our cause. We join with you, the people of India, and with people all over the world in our striving towards a new tomorrow, tomorrow making a reality for all mankind the sort of universe that the great Rabindranath Tagore dreamed of in *Gitanjali:*

"Where the mind is without fear and the head is held high, where knowledge is free;
where the world has not been broken into
fragments by narrow domestic walls;
where words came out from the depths of truth;
where tireless striving stretches its arms towards perfection;
where the clear stream of reason has not lost
its way into the dreary desert sand of dead habit;
where the mind is led forward by these into
ever widening thought and action
into that haven of Freedom, My Father, let my country awake."

Yours sincerely,

August 3, 1982   (Signed) NELSON MANDELA

Mrs. Manorama Bhalla
Secretary
Indian Council for Cultural Relations
Indraprastha Estate
New Delhi
Republic of India

P.S. As will be seen from the above date, the letter was given to the Officer Commanding Robben Island on the 3rd August

1980 for despatch to you by mail. I added that the matter should be treated urgently. Since then I have repeatedly enquired from the Department of Prisons as to whether the letter had been forwarded to you. Only during the last week in December was I told that I "could thank the Indian Council for Cultural Relations but not in the words used in the letter." For this reason I decided to use my own channels of reaching you.

NELSON MANDELA'S STATEMENTS
IN THE COURT

"How can I be expected to believe that this same racial discrimination, which has been the cause of so much injustice and suffering right through the years, should now operate here to give me a fair and open trial?

"I consider myself neither morally nor legally obliged to obey laws made by a Parliament in which I am not represented. That the will of the people is the basis of the authority of government is a principle universally acknowledged as sacred throughout the civilized world."

*   *   *

"I hate race discrimination most intensely and in all its manifestations. I have fought it all my life; I fight it now, and will do so until the end of my days. Even although I now happen to be tried by one, whose opinion I hold in high esteem, I detest most violently the set-up that surrounds me here. It makes me feel that I am a Black man in a White man's court. This should not be. I should feel perfectly at ease and at home with the assurance that I am being tried by a fellow South African, who does not regard me as an inferior, entitled to a special type of justice."

*   *   *

"I hate the practice of race discrimination, and in my hatred, I am sustained by the fact that the overwhelming majority of mankind hate it equally. I hate the systematic inclusion of children with colour prejudice and I am sustained in that hatred by the fact that the overwhelming majority of mankind, here and abroad, are with me in that. I hate the racial arrogance which decrees that the good things of life shall be retained as the exclusive right of a minority of the population, confining the majority to a position of subservience and inferiority, and maintaining them as voteless chattels to work, where they are told and behave as they are told by the ruling minority. I am sustained in that hatred by the fact that the overwhelming majority of mankind both in this country and abroad are with me. Nothing that this court can do to me will change in any way that hatred in me, which can only be removed by the removal of the injustice and inhumanity, which I have sought to remove from the political, social and economic life of this country.

"Whatever sentence Your Worship sees fit to impose upon me for the crime for which I have been convicted before this court, may it rest assured that when my sentence has been completed, I will still be moved, as men are always moved, by their conscience. I will still be moved by my dislike of the race discrimination against my people. When I come out from serving my sentence, I will take up again, as best I can, the struggle for the removal of those injustices until they are finally abolished once and for all."

MANDELA, TAMBO AND ANC:
EPG REPORT

"Mission to South Africa: The Commonwealth Report" as the book is called is more widely known as the "EPG Report" or "Commonwealth Group of Eminent Persons' Report," from which some extracts about Nelson Mandela, Oliver Tambo and the ANC are reproduced here.

In 1985, at the Commonwealth Summit at Nassau in the Bahamas, the Heads of State or Government of 49 Commonwealth countries decided on exerting pressure for change in South Africa and appointed the Commonwealth Group of Eminent Persons to prepare a comprehensive report on South Africa.

The seven eminent members of the Group were Malcolm Fraser (Co-Chairman) former Prime Minister of Australia, General Olusegun Obasanjo (Co-Chairman), former Head of State of Nigeria, Lord Barber of Wentbridge, former Chancellor of Exchequer, Britain (and Chairman of the Standard Chartered Bank), Dame Nita Barrow, Co-President of World Council of Churches, Barbados (and former President of YWCA), John Malecela, former Foreign Minister of Tanzania, Sardar Swaran Singh of India, who has held several portfolios as a Central Minister (External Affairs, Defence, etc from 1952 onwards) and the Most Reverend Edward Walter Scott, Archbishop of the Anglican Church of Canada.

The EPG Report was completed in mid-1986 and since then it has been widely circulated. It has been published by Penguin Books for the Commonwealth Secretariat. The Report has paid high tribute to Mandela, Tambo and the

ANC. Extracts are reproduced here courtesy Commonwealth Secretariat.

The Release of Nelson Mandela and others
(*From Chapter 3*)

From the beginning, we recognized the essential significance in any political settlement of one man — Nelson Mandela. Imprisoned these last twenty-four years, latterly in Pollsmoor Prison, he is an isolated and lonely figure, bearing his incarceration with courage and fortitude, anxious to be reunited with his wife and family, but determined that this can only be in circumstances which allow for his unconditional release, along with colleagues and fellow political prisoners, and permit them all to take part in normal political activity.

A symbol to many, Nelson Mandela can be said to represent all those imprisoned, detained, banned or in exile for their opposition to apartheid: men like Wilton Mcquai, Govan Mbeki, Zephania Mothupeng and John Ganya on Robben Island; Walter Sisulu, Ahmed Kathrada, Raymond Mhlaba, Andrew Mlangeni and Oscar Mpetha, also in Pollsmoor; Elias Matsoaledi and Harry Gwala in Johannesburg; Patrick Lekota and Popo Molefe in Modderbee; and many others. Certainly, that was the hope expressed by him in the statement, conveyed by his daughter, Miss Zindzi Mandela, to a meeting at the Jabulani Amphitheatre on February 10, 1985. The general question of political trials and the release of detainees is one we will return to later in our Report.

Mr. Mandela is himself a political prisoner. In 1964, he and nine others were convicted on a charge of sabotage. In his statement from the dock at the Rivonia Trial, he set out the reasons which led him to do what he did — the lengths to which the ANC had gone to avoid violence since its inception in 1912 and the repressive policies upholding apartheid which, he argued, had finally forced upon them a reactive violence.

He told the court that when the ANC had been declared an unlawful organization, it had refused to dissolve and had gone underground. It was only after that, in June 1961, that he had come to the conclusion that violence was inevitable and that it would be unrealistic and wrong for African leaders to continue with a policy of non-violence, when the Government had 'met our demands with violence.' Thereafter, it was decided that the ANC would 'no longer disapprove of properly controlled sabotage,' by which means the economy would be damaged and international attention attracted. He remains deprived of his liberty because he is not prepared to disavow that decision. As he himself has put it: 'I am in prison as the representative of the people and the African National Congress, which was banned. What freedom am I being offered, while the organization of the people remains banned?' (Statement, February 10, 1985.)

But Nelson Mandela is also a symbol for Blacks not only of their lack of political freedom but also of their struggle to attain it. He is a potent inspiration for much of the political activity of Black South Africans. His role in the management of the Defiance Campaign of 1952 and his leadership of Umkhonto we Sizwe (Spear of the Nation), for which he remains imprisoned, together with the manner in which he has borne his fate, have established him as a legend in his own lifetime. His suffering is seen as the suffering of all who are the victims of apartheid. The campaign for his release has been the galvanizing spur for rising Black political consciousness across South Africa. His name is emblazoned across the length and breadth of Black South Africa.

In particular, the call for his freedom has developed into the centrepiece of the demand for a political settlement. It is the shorthand for the proposition that, as his daughter Zindzi conveyed it, 'There is an alternative to the inevitable bloodbath.'

But we also recognize that, for some Whites, he represents something rather different. Their fears, if unfounded, are real nonetheless. They include the belief that Nelson Mandela is a man of violence and that violence could not be contained on his release; the fear that, as one of the principal Black nationalists, his sole aim is to achieve a hand-over of state power from White to Black; and the fear that his release would be the signal for chaos and destruction. Most of these fears have been fuelled by the Government's own campaign against Mr. Mandela and the

ANC. To that extent, they are self-induced, but they are real for all that and cannot be ignored.

Nelson Mandela has indeed become a living legend. Just as the gaoling of nationalist leaders like Mahatma Gandhi and Jomo Kenyatta invested them with a unique aura and helped galvanize resistance to the colonial power, so, we believe, the imprisonment of Nelson Mandela is a self-defeating course for the South African Government to take.

With each month and year of further incarceration, the difficulties of the Government will grow. While fit at present, he is a man of 67. It would be wise to heed the words of Soren Kierkegaard: 'The tyrant dies and his rule ends: the martyr dies and his rule begins.'

Discussions with Nelson Mandela were obviously going to be essential to our work. Initially, arranging such discussions did not prove easy. Other visiting groups had been denied access, and the South African authorities approached our request with great caution. We also asked to see other political prisoners and detainees in Pollsmoor and on Robben Island.

During the preliminary visit, General Obasanjo was permitted to see Mr Mandela. Thereafter, the full Group met with him on two occasions, although not with other detainees. In all these meetings we were conscious of our responsibility to Nelson Mandela himself. As recently as February 10, 1985, when referring to suggestions for his conditional release, he had referred to the constraints that custody imposes: 'Only free men can negotiate,' he said, 'prisoners cannot enter into contracts.' It was essential, we felt, that we should meet and talk with him. We were equally determined that those conversations should neither compromise nor embarrass him. We reiterate that intent in drawing on those conversations for the purposes of our Report.

The Group approached the meetings with Mr Mandela with another measure of care. It was impossible not to be aware of the mythology surrounding him, but, equally, we were determined that it should not colour our impressions or influence our judgement. As far as possible, we resolved to approach these meetings with an open mind.

63

We were *first* struck by his physical authority — by his immaculate appearance, his apparent good health and his commanding presence. In his manner he exuded authority and received the respect of all around him, including his gaolers. That in part seemed to reflect his own philosophy of separating people from policy.

His authority clearly extends throughout the nationalist movement, although he constantly reiterated that he could not speak for his colleagues in the ANC, that, apart from his personal viewpoint, any concerted view must come after proper consultation with all concerned and that his views could carry weight only when expressed collectively through the ANC.

There was no visible distance of outlook, however, between Nelson Mandela and the ANC leadership in Lusaka. He was at pains to point out that his own authority derived solely from his position within the organization, and in so far as he was able to reflect the popular will.

Second, we found his attitude to others outside the ANC reasonable and conciliatory. He did not conceal his differences with Chief Buthelezi, and he was conscious of the divisions which had arisen among the Black community. Nevertheless, he was confident that, if he were to be released from prison, the unity of all Black leaders, including Chief Buthelezi, could be achieved. The ANC, as the vanguard of the liberation movement, had particular responsibilities, but the fact that freedom fighters belonged to a variety of organizations was both a challenge to, and an indictment of, the ANC. He stressed repeatedly the importance of the unity of the whole nationalist movement.

In our discussions, Nelson Mandela also took care to emphasize his desire for reconciliation across the divide of colour. He described himself as a deeply committed South African nationalist but added that South African nationalists came in more than one colour — there were White people, Coloured People and Indian people who were also deeply committed South African nationalists. He pledged himself anew to work for a multi-racial society in which all would have a secure place.

He recognized the fears of many White people, which had been intensified by the Government's own propaganda, but emphasized the importance of minority groups being given a real sense of security in any new society in South Africa.

That desire for goodwill was palpable. The Minister of Justice, together with two senior officials, was present at the start of our second meeting and Mr Mandela pressed him to remain, saying he had nothing to hide and no objection to the Minister hearing the discussion. It was his strongly stated view that if the circumstances could be created in which the Government and the ANC could talk, some of the problems, which arose solely through lack of contact could be eliminated. The fact of talking was essential in the building of mutual confidence.

Third, we were impressed by the consistency of his beliefs. He emphasized that he was a nationalist, not a Communist, and that his principles were unchanged from those to which he subscribed, when the Freedom Charter was drawn up in 1955. Those principles included the necessity for the unity and political emancipation of all Africans in the land of their birth; the need for a multi-racial society, free from any kind of racial, religious or political discrimination; the paramountcy of democratic principles and of political and human rights; and equality of opportunity. He held to the view that the Freedom Charter embodied policies, which amounted to a devastating attack on discrimination in all its ramifications — economic, social and political.

While it called for a new order, this was not to be on the basis of any change in the system of production apart from certain key sectors. He argued that he and his colleagues had been to court because of the Freedom Charter, that the court had deliberated for four years before giving its verdict that the Crown had failed to establish its case, and the Freedom Charter was not a document designed to establish even socialism in South Africa. He recognized it was a document, which some might not consider 'progressive' enough; it was nonetheless one to which he still subscribed and which, he believed, could have a wide appeal to Whites as well as to Blacks.

Our *fourth* impressioi. was that Nelson Mandela was a man who had been driven to armed struggle only with the greatest reluctance, solely in the absence of any other alternative to the violence of the apartheid system, and never as an end in itself. It was a course of action, which he argued had been forced upon him, as he explained at his trial in 1964: 'A time comes in the life of any nation, when there remains only two choices—submit or fight. That time has now come to South Africa. We shall not submit and we have no choice but to hit back by all the means in our power in defence of our people, our future and our freedom.'

At that trial, he had gone to great lengths to show that Umkhonto we Sizwe's policy was to avoid hurting civilians and instead to concentrate on damaging property. That policy was apparently maintained until 1983, when the ANC's first car bomb exploded at Air Force Headquarters in Pretoria. Yet Mr Mandela even then had expressed his sadness over the incident and had said from prison: 'It was a tragic accident ... we aim for buildings and property. It might be that someone gets killed in the fire, in the heat of battle, but we do not believe in assassination.'

We questioned Nelson Mandela extensively about his views on violence. The ANC, he said, had for many years operated as a non-violent organization and had been forced into armed struggle only because it became the unavoidable response to the violence of apartheid. He stressed that violence could never be an ultimate solution and that the nature of human relationships required negotiation. He was not in a position to renounce the use of violence as a condition of his release, and we recognized that in the circumstances currently prevailing in South Africa it would be unreasonable to expect that of him or anyone else.

Fifth, there was no doubting Nelson Mandela's welcome for the Commonwealth initiative and his personal desire to help. While emphasizing that he could not speak for the ANC, he expressed his personal acceptance of the Group's negotiating concept as a starting point. He made it clear that his personal acceptance stood, regardless of whether or not it was acceptable to the South African Government, but he wanted his views to be those of the movement and not simply his own, and there would be need for consultation with his fellow prisoners (both in Pollsmoor and on Robben Island) and with the ANC in Lusaka.

He believed that if a positive response by the ANC and the Government were to be synchronized — the Government withdrawing the army and the police from the townships and taking other agreed steps, while the ANC agreed, at the same time, to a suspension of violence and to negotiations — there should be no difficulty with implementation. He acknowledged, however, that his release would not be enough to lessen violence. He and his colleagues would have to take on the active role of persuading people to call off violent activities and to respect the negotiating process. This meant that the negotiating process had to be fully credible and kept so by the Government.

Our *sixth*, and final, impression was of a man, who yearned for his freedom and who longed to be reunited with his family, but who would never accept it under what he called 'humiliating conditions.' As he put it in his statement of February 10, 1985:

"I cherish my own freedom dearly, but I care even more for your freedom. Too many have died since I went to prison. Too many have suffered for the love of freedom. I owe it to their widows, to their orphans, to their mothers and their fathers, who have grieved and wept for them.

"Not only have I suffered during these long lonely wasted years. I am no less life-loving than you are. But I cannot sell the birthright of the people to be free.

"Only free men can negotiate. Prisoners cannot enter into contracts. Your freedom and mine cannot be separated."

We accept that the release on Nelson Mandela presents the South African Government with a difficult dilemma. Having held him too long in prison, there is a growing realization in Government circles that any benefits of incarceration are outweighed by the disadvantages, which daily become more apparent. Yet to release him now, as some in Government say is their wish, would be to do so into conditions much changed from ten, or even five, years ago. In a mood of unrest and upheaval, with growing Black awareness and political protest being matched by increasing anxiety among Whites and the rise of White extremism, the Government has expressed the fear that his release might result in an uncontrollable explosion of violence.

We do not hold this view. Provided the negotiating process were agreed, Mr Mandela's own voice would appeal for calm. We believe his authority would secure it.

In our discussions with the ANC, it has become clear that they, along with every Black group within South Africa, see the unconditional release of Nelson Mandela and other political prisoners and detainees as a necessary and crucial step towards a settlement. Negotiations cannot take place in the absence of the people's authentic leaders. The release into South African society of those leaders would lead logically to negotiations, through a process of normal political activity, on behalf of legally recognized organizations. No other equation is possible. No piecemeal or more limited approach can possibly succeed.

Without this first step, linked to a wider package, the ANC and others will have no basis for believing in the state violence of the apartheid system ever abating and will not be persuaded to suspend violence themselves. The struggle and the killing will continue with greater intensity. The cycle of violence will remain unbroken.

Mr Mandela, according to all the evidence, is a unifying, commanding and popular leader. Recent opinion polls, as well as our personal observations, revealed that Blacks, Indians and Coloureds look overwhelmingly to Nelson Mandela as the leader of a non-racial South Africa.

To disregard Nelson Mandela, by continuing his imprisonment, would be to discard an essential and heroic figure in any political settlement in South Africa. His freedom is a key component in any hope of a peaceful resolution of a conflict which otherwise will prove all-consuming.

68

The African National Congress (ANC)

(From Chapter 5)

In assessing the position of the ANC and its leadership, several factors need to be taken into account, namely that the ANC is a banned organization in South Africa; that Nelson Mandela and many others of its leadership have been imprisoned for almost a quarter of a century; that the ANC and its objectives enjoy considerable popular support among Black South Africans; and that the role of its external leadership and the nature of the ANC struggle are central to the South African political problem.

The Government acknowledged that we would need to consult with the ANC leadership both within and outside South Africa. It facilitated our meetings with Nelson Mandela in Pollsmoor Prison on three occasions.

Close contacts were established at an early stage with the ANC's external leadership, which led to two formal consultations with ANC President, Oliver Tambo and members of the ANC Executive in Lusaka.

The ANC leadership told us that their immediate reaction to the setting up of the Group had been one of disappointment. Their hopes had been raised by the debate in Nassau and the prospect of increased international pressure on the Government through sanctions against Pretoria. Instead, the Group had been established and, in their view, it would assist in relieving the pressures on the South African Government, which had been building up in the period before Nassau. We were nevertheless warmly welcomed as the ANC had a keen interest in hearing what the Group felt it might be able to do.

In the ANC's view, a peaceful resolution of the crisis in South Africa would become possible if the Government took immediately the steps elaborated in the Nassau Accord. These coincided with what the people of South Africa had been demanding for many years — but to date it appeared that the Botha regime was interested not in negotiations but only in pursuing a war against the people. Dialogue of a kind had also been going on for many years — but statements and counter-statements were not enough. Negotiations went beyond dialogue and should address the essential issue, the elimination of apartheid.

In the ANC analysis, the Government was projecting itself as embarking on a process of reform because of the pressures it was under. These sprang from various sources: the continuing threat of further sanctions and the growing sense of isolation from the international community was one; the escalating conflict and violence, which had developed a momentum of its own, was another. Both would be crucial determinants of change. Immense pressure would be required before the South African Government would be ready to negotiate seriously. At the moment, the Government purported to be promoting dialogue by establishing a National Statutory Council as an alternative to the fourth Chamber of Parliament, but it would be a consultative body without power. Along with the Tricameral Parliament, it had been rejected by the people because it was not what they were demanding — liberation from racist oppression, full political power and full political rights.

The ANC expressed great interest in the South African Government's response to our mandate, because only then would it be able to make its own contribution. If the Government was prepared to shift its ground and indicate its readiness for fundamental change this would impact on the ANC view. Their assessment was, however, that nothing had changed and nothing would change. If that proved to be the case, then the conditions for negotiation did not exist.

The ANC placed much emphasis on the release of Nelson Mandela, a crucial step, which recognized that it was not possible for negotiation to take place in the absence of the people's authentic leaders. A pre-requisite for talking to the Government was that it should be through the people's recognized leaders, not through the ones the Government chose to identify. Without this essential first step, the conflict would continue.

On the question of violence, the ANC expressed concern that the situation as it had developed over the years was one of conflict and violence escalating and developing a momentum of

70

its own. This likelihood had been foreseen as early as the 1950s by the ANC, namely that the violence of the apartheid regime would eventually drive South African people to resort to violence themselves in self-defence.

We questioned them particularly about the possibility of a suspension of violence on both sides leading towards cessation. The ANC's response was that it was important to understand the nature of the violence, how it came about, who started it and how the others had reacted. The introduction of apartheid in 1948 had heralded an era of unprecedented violence by the South African State. The ANC's response had been to counter-act government-sponsored violence with a campaign of non-violence, which had been pursued throughout the 1950s, despite the employment of increased violence by the South African Government to restrict the ANC and to stifle Black rights. This culminated at the end of the 1950s with Sharpeville and a calamitous decade of killing.

Still the ANC persisted with its policy of non-violence. It was only in 1961, when the army was deployed in a massive way, nationwide, to stamp out a peaceful strike organized by Nelson Mandela, that the ANC decided that it was necessary to embark on an armed struggle. Despite this, over the past twenty years or so the ANC said it had been very selective in its targets and the number of deaths resulting from ANC activities was hardly twenty. In one single incident in Soweto about a thousand children were shot at indiscriminately by the security forces.

Violence in South Africa was attributed as being the result of the apartheid system which needed guns, arrests and prisons to maintain it; violence would abate if the system was dismantled. With the abandonment of apartheid the way would open for a cessation of violence on both sides. If the army and the police pulled out of the townships, the ANC could begin to consider a suspension of violence.

In any event, the ANC's stand on violence did not mean there could not be serious negotiation. There were many instances of negotiation taking place to end hostilities, as had been the case in Zimbabwe. There were other cases directly involving the South African Government in negotiation in the midst of conflict and fighting, as in Mozambique and Angola. If the conditions set out in the Nassau Accord were fulfilled by the South African Government and if there were seen to be prospects for resolving fundamental issues* within a short period, it would go a long way in demonstrating that there was no need for violence and help to reduce the level of the armed struggle. It was conceivable that the struggle could be called off altogether. But before that stage was reached, the ANC could hardly be expected to act unilaterally. For the ANC to renounce violence now would be to reduce itself to a state of helplessness. There must first be sufficient indications of the South African Government's readiness to negotiate the transition to non-racial sovereignty.

The ANC counselled us against being drawn into a situation with the Government where, as with the Contact Group on Namibia, there were continually postponed decisions and deferred expectations. Its assessment was that the South African Government's declarations of reform had shown no evidence of a preparedness to undertake the fundamental changes that were being demanded. There had been no real departures in policy, only an attempt to lull opposition forces into inactivity and to consolidate White minority rule. In the circumstances, we were urged to adhere to our six-month timetable and not be drawn into playing a game in which it would appear that the South African Government was beginning a process and at the same time allowing time to slip by. By taking a firm stand and adhering to our timetable the real intentions of the South African Government in respect of negotiations would be tested.

Meeting with ANC Representatives in Lusaka

(*From Chapter 6*)

We travelled to Lusaka to brief the ANC leadership on progress and to share the negotiating concept with them. We reported that the concept had been with the Government for more than two months and that we had deliberately not revealed it to the ANC until this juncture because we had seen little point in discussing it with them prior to receiving positive indications from the Government. The Government, while indicating that it was considering it seriously, had not yet said either 'yes' or 'no'. Its acceptance would involve the Government in doing a great deal to prove its sincerity and genuineness in wanting a negotiated solution. Our consultations with Nelson Mandela had been extensive but he had emphasized that in reacting favourably to the concept as a starting point he was speaking as an individual. He had stressed that, if there was to be a considered reaction from him, it would be necessary for him to consult with his ANC colleagues. We informed them that we had urged strongly upon the Government that Mr Mandela's proposal for consultations with fellow ANC prisoners and others inside the country be allowed.

Mr Tambo, ANC President, said it was not going to be possible to give a considered response straight away. He noted that the South African Government, after all these weeks, had still not given the Group a substantive answer. The ANC was in a far more difficult position than the Government. It was based in Lusaka in exile; the organization was spread out; it had responsibilities to many people, including leaders in jail and all those within South Africa, who supported its endeavours and influenced its thinking.

By way of initial reaction, however, he was in a position to say that in so far as the concept corresponded to the principles and requirements of the Nassau Accord, it would command the support of the ANC.

Mr Tambo said the ANC had no objection to negotiations and would participate in them so long as they were proper and honest, and not just a device to quell internal demands and weaken external pressures. The ANC could never forget that they were dealing with a regime which did not honour its undertakings and was a master of prevarication. When the South African Government said it wanted negotiations, the question arose whether it was honest in its intentions. Had Pretoria not negotiated with the South West African People's Organization (SWAPO) and the Contact Group for eight long years? Had it not negotiated with Mozambique and Angola and signed agreements which it had then proceeded to violate from the very outset?

There was, thus, a need for the South African Government to demonstrate its good faith, and for the Group to apply the acid test to satisfy itself that the Government was ready for negotiations. No negotiations could be fruitful if there were the slightest reservations in the mind of the Government about the dismantling of apartheid or 'erecting the structures of democracy' as stated in the Nassau Accord.

Members of the ANC Executive sought a number of specific clarifications. For example, the concept could be interpreted as implying that the removal of the military from the townships would itself result in freedom of assembly and discussion. It would be helpful to know what the Group really meant. We clarified that these were separate thoughts: the Government was being asked both to remove the military from the townships and, additionally, to create conditions for freedom of assembly and discussion.

The ANC also wished to know what was meant by the phrase 'power-sharing.' If this were a code word for potential Black participation in the racist Tricameral Constitution and its institutions, there would be no basis for a negotiation. We explained that the Government had given an assurance that the agenda would be an open one and that how the balance was struck on the question of power-sharing would be a matter for the negotiations themselves.

On the issue of violence, we clarified that the steps required of the Government would amount to a suspension of the violence of the apartheid system, and it was only in that context that a corresponding suspension of violence by the ANC was being sought. We had made it clear to the Government that it would be unrealistic and impracticable to expect the ANC to renounce violence for all time, regardless of the success or failure of negotiations, nor would we be prepared to endorse any such demand by the Government.

Mr Tambo affirmed the ANC and the Group had a common interest in reaching a point where all could say that apar-

74

theid was no more. The ANC appreciated that the concept contained within it the possibility of getting them to that position. He and his colleagues would want about ten days for consultations before giving a firm answer to the Group.

On this encouraging basis we returned to South Africa, having agreed to the possibility of a further round of talks with the ANC in Lusaka in the first week of June (1986) in the light of the Government's response.

WE ARE OF THE WORLD AND
THE WORLD IS WITH US

TAMBO'S ACCEPTANCE SPEECH AT
JAWAHARLAL NEHRU UNIVERSITY, NEW DELHI

Here is the full text of the address by Oliver Tambo in response to the conferment on him of the degree of Doctorate of Laws *honoris causa* by the Jawaharlal Nehru University, New Delhi, on May 9, 1986. He had come to India on an official visit at the invitation of the Government of India.

Today, I stand before this august and eminent assembly to receive an honorary degree of Doctor of Laws. The question I have pondered without results from the day, I first learnt of this possibility and since my arrival in this country three days ago, when I learnt of this occasion, has been decided: Why me? Why pick on me? In what way do I, more than other South Africans, more than other political leaders and activists of yesterday today, and tomorrow, deserve to be honoured with a Doctorate by any university, least of all by one that carries the immortal name of Jawaharlal Nehru?

For, the struggle against the inhumanity that apartheid has featured many great men and women, whose contribution to the common effort has been, and in numerous cases, continues to be the most outstanding. Today, that struggle involves as active participants not only the vast majority of the people of South Africa of all races, but also the people of the entire region of Southern Africa. It involves peoples in Africa and world-wide.

76

We know that we shall win because we are of the world and the world is with us.

Considering my own relatively meagre contribution in the face of this massive popular effort, it can only be with great humility, even with reluctance, that I accept the honour you have bestowed on me. But allow me to accept it in the name of the youth and the children of South Africa, who have not left it to their parents and professors to fight for their future, but have themselves joined that fight with breath-taking courage.

The present phase of the South African struggle can be traced back to several historic events, starting with the landing of Jan Van Riebeeck in South Africa in 1652. Or, we could look at the consequences for Southern Africa and the international community of the remarkably racist constitution forced on the majority of the people of South Africa by the British Government in 1910. That constitution, as racist today as it was then, provided, in the interim period, fertile ground for the development in our society of ideas borrowed from Hitler's National Socialism — ideas which, ironically, found vigorous expression and implementation in South Africa even as Nazism lay in smouldering ruins in Germany. The battle-front in the defence of democracy had changed its form and its location. The onslaught came not from Nazism but from something called apartheid, with its operational base, not in Germany but in Pretoria. Its objective was to conquer and subdue the whole of South Africa and then spread its domain over the rest of the African continent.

Looking back over the past four decades of apartheid rule, the most striking feature is the massive destruction of human life and property covering the whole region of Southern Africa, Quite clearly, the operation of the apartheid system is an act of war, and has the consequences that attach to any war — massive destruction of human life and national property.

The 1910 South Africa Constitution, enforced and defended by racists of the purest blood, stands at the heart of an on-going war and continuing acts and threats of destabilisation in different parts of Southern Africa. The question whether marriages are mixed or unmixed is of no consequence. Nor does it matter any longer that a law is removed from or added to the Statute Book. The fundamental question today is: Who does the removing or adding and on what authority? The legitimacy of the apartheid regime is being called in question.

The central issue is the inalienable right of the people of South Africa together to exercise full and untramelled power over the affairs of their country, on the basis of a new and fully democratic fundamental law or constitution which, as envisaged in our Freedom Charter, will destroy the apartheid system in all its ramifications and manifestations. For the African National Congress (ANC) and the popular masses in South Africa, there is only one road to such a constitution: It is the hard and bitter road of resolute and relentless struggle — a road which "is no easy walk to freedom," as Nelson Mandela said, quoting Jawaharlal Nehru.

We know however, from the inspiring example of India under the illustrious leadership of Mahatma Gandhi and Jawaharlal Nehru, that the road is feasible and freedom attainable. Our hearts across the ocean, in the ghettoes of racist South Africa, leapt with joy; we shared with you the ecstasy of that rare moment when, at the stroke of the midnight hour on August 15, 1947, Pandit Nehru spoke of the epic Indian freedom struggle, the "tryst with destiny" many of you had the great sacrifices made in the course of that struggle, and your determination at the hour of victory to build a peaceful, free and prosperous society. In these words, Pandit Nehru articulated our own aspirations and India filled us with expectations of imminent freedom.

What we did not know in August 1947 was that barely nine months later, a force sweeping with unprecedented violence in the direction opposed to the march of history was to unleash itself on the people of South Africa. It was just as well that India had by her victory lifted the momentum of our struggle in South Africa and given us a sense of triumph. This enabled us to take on the apartheid onslaught.

But even before her independence, India had prepared the

international community to rise to the challenge of apartheid by planting the issue of segregation at the United Nations.

Since 1947, most of the colonised world has joined the community of free, sovereign and independent nations. Of equal importance, the issue of segregation, later apartheid, has become a household issue around the world.

All this speaks most eloquently of the centrality of India's enduring and supportive role in the long and gruelling but heroic struggle of the people of South Africa and Southern Africa to end a crime against humanity, of which Britain cannot in the final analysis claim innoncence.

But how far have we travelled towards the attainment of this noble goal. Today, a part of myself is on Robben Island and Poolsmoor, where hundreds who have given up their liberty in the cause of peace are confined; a part of me is among the street and area committees of Port Alfred, Mamelodi, Alexandra Township; a part is in the bowels of the earth, among the Black diggers of gold that pays for the guns that kill miners' mothers and children in Southern Africa. Yet, a part of me is among the broad masses comprising all colours, marching confidently along the tunnel of progress at the end of which a glow of light has appeared. After decades of darkness, there is light; the end is in sight, whatever the intervening distance in terms of measurable progress. The light is there for all to see, Pretoria not excluded. The latter will seek to buy precious time and postpone the demise of apartheid and White minority rule by taking recourse to massacres within and outside South Africa. But it is not for want of brutal repression that we have reached this far, after decades of permanent violence.

Now that the victims of the apartheid crime can both sense and see the goal of their sacrifices, nothing on earth can, and nothing will stop them. But they seek nothing beyond a South Africa that will truly belong to all who live in it, and would rather that the new order in South Africa were born now rather than later and without violence, if the apartheid system were capable of non-violence, which it is not.

It is in this context that the question of a "negotiated settlement" arises. At the moment, the Eminent Persons Group set up by the Commonwealth Heads of State and Government has started a process of negotiations with the Pretoria regime, which should hopefully clear the way for negotiations between Pretoria and the leadership of the broad democratic movement headed by ANC. The indications are that the first set of negotiations are likely to be protracted beyond the envisaged six months. If the experience of Namibia is anything to go by, the second set of negotiations will be put on an endless road if they should see the light of day.

The danger—and Pretoria's intention is to shift the focus of world attention from the ongoing crime against humanity and the urgent need to stop it, to an endless dialogue during the course of which, to the delight of the defenders of the criminal system, international pressures fall out of fashion, while the butchery, in the interests of "law and order" proceeds unabated. For what other reasons does the apartheid regime put out unrealistic conditions, which include a demand that the Western powers should guarantee its right to perpetrate massacres against the people demanding an end to the apartheid system? Significantly, Botha already sees the imposition of sanctions as being contingent, not upon the persistence of the apartheid crime, but only upon extreme instances of carnage such as massacres.

It is the hope of the ANC and the daily victims of the apartheid system that as we sustain and intensify our own struggle, the international community will respond appropriately to its responsibilities. It is indeed our firm belief that inasmuch as our struggle is against human enslavement, against racial tyranny and oppression, against exploitation and human degradation, for the creation of a new socio-political and economic order in our country, it is part of the world-wide struggle for freedom, justice and peace, all of which demand sustained and determined action.

It is in this context that we look with confidence, firstly to the Brussels Conference on Namibia, which started early this week, secondly, to the World Conference on Sanctions scheduled to take place in Paris next month, and the great Summit of the Non-Aligned Movement in Harare later in the year. The cumulative effect of these powerful forces on the fortunes and misfortunes of the Pretoria regime, on the issue of sanctions and other international pressures should mark a distinct turning point in the fortunes of apartheid.

This is not an issue I need belabour before any audience in India. I mention it at some length because it is a matter of serious concern to all concerned: to all active opponents of the apartheid system, because they seek its speediest demise; to the Pretoria regime because sanctions threaten its survival, and to the regime's allies because sanction will help to liberate Black workers from the excesses of apartheid exploitation and take away from these allies a most lucrative source of profits.

You have honoured me with a Doctorate in law. You might have expected me to reflect on the subject in the course of response. But South African law as it effects the majority of the South African population is apartheid law. It expresses itself in and secures the effective operation of the apartheid system.

For all the indisputable eminence of South Africa's jurists as men or women of law, if the system of laws wherewith they practice their calling is founded on naked injustice, is conceived and enforced to serve the ends of injustice, the courts of law which purport to apply that law become instruments in the hands of injustice. Whereas, as in South Africa, the over-riding preoccupation of the law-makers is what we have all come to identify as the apartheid system, then to talk of "law and order" as relating to the victim of the system is to stand reality on its head, for in that situation, for the Black persons and other members of the oppressed majority, their reality is total lawlessness and disorder experienced at the hands of the apartheid regime.

Let me conclude by recalling that in 1980, I stood in this same hall to receive, on behalf of Nelson Mandela, the Jawaharlal Nehru Award for International Understanding and Peace (1979). I his letter of acceptance, smuggled out of Robben Island, where he was imprisoned at the time, Mandela spoke of the great impact the Indian freedom struggle had made on him, and in particular the impact of the lives of Mahatma

Gandhi and Pandit Nehru. Mandela spoke for Walter Sisulu, Ahmed Kathrada, Dorothy Nyembck and every other activist of our struggle. Today, we must add another pillar of strength, who continued firmly in the tradition set by her predecessors — she, whose gentle and soothing voice we can hear no more, although her message rings loud and clear as ever before in South Africa — Indira Gandhi.

I wish your prestigious and renowned university continuing success in its endeavour to enrich your great country in various fields of human activity. And to the fraternal leaders and people of India, our best wishes for peace and prosperity.

TIME INDEED IS RUNNING OUT

Extract from the address by Oliver Tambo to the Paris Sanctions Conference June 16, 1986.

Surely, it has by now become patently clear to all thinking people that unless the world takes decisive action now, a bloodbath in South and Southern Africa is inevitable. Death, which has become our daily bread in South Africa, has also become so much a part of our lives that it can no longer serve as deterrence discouraging struggle. The urgent necessity to end the murderous system of apartheid presses on us with the greatest insistence. And, therefore, having learnt the lessons that the enemy seeks to teach us today, our people will join the armed offensive in even greater numbers, displaying the same bravery and the same contempt for death that they have shown in the last two years and before.

We speak not with a sense of satisfaction, when we say that the Botha regime has dragged our country into the situation, which we witness today. The prospect of growing numbers of people killed and injured, be they Black or White, does not fill us with any joy. We view it as a sombre prospect and wish it could have been avoided.

However, we have learnt to look at reality in the face. That reality demands that in order to win our liberty, we must be prepared to make the necessary sacrifices. It also demands that we should steel ourselves for war with all the consequences which that implies.

We are certainly not prepared to live as slaves and will, therefore, continue to intensify our offensive for the victory of the cause of democracy, national liberation and peace in our country.

The certainty of greatly increased violence is not confined to South Africa. It is a prospect which faces the peoples of Southern Africa. Already, many people have died in our region and enormous destruction has been caused by the aggression of the apartheid regime. Many people are dying now and destruction is in process. As the regime grows more desperate, so will it seek to wreak more havoc throughout the region.

The major Western powers and, in particular, the United States, Great Britain, the Federal Republic of Germany, as well as others, cannot avoid taking the blame for this inevitable and terrible outcome. It is they who have, above all, shielded the apartheid regime from decisive international action. They have aided and abetted this regime in the past and continue to do so today. Current reports confirm that these governments remain determined to persist in their ignoble and dishonourable role as allies of a truly murderous regime.

It has been our fervent hope that these governments would have drawn the necessary conclusions from the report of the Commonwealth Group of Eminent Persons. Moved by what it saw and heard in South Africa, the Group of Eminent Persons has given timely warning about the impending, horrendous blood-bath and called for decisive action by the international community to avert this possibility.

Of necessity, this call is directed in the first instance to the principal economic partners of apartheid South Africa—the countries we have already mentioned. It is one of the great tragedies of our epoch that countries, which see themselves as the most exemplary democracies of all time should choose to go down in history as the force that blocked the birth of democracy in South Africa and elected instead to appease racism and White minority rule and consequently to see our people perish in their millions.

Time is indeed running out, if it has not done so already. If those who have the power and obligation to impose sanctions fail to do so now, then history will surely judge them as co-conspirators and participants in the commission of a crime of immense dimensions.

The African National Congress, and the masses of the people

it leads, are committed to the victory of the cause of democracy in our country. There should be no doubt whatsoever that with your support, we shall emerge victorious. Already, reports coming out of South Africa today confirm that despite all the extraordinary measures of state terrorism that the Botha regime has adopted, our people, as we have said, have moved to demonstrate their determination to bring this regime down.

These masses, and their organisations, the ANC and other democratic forces, would dearly love to liberate our country from a racist tyranny by peaceful means, including negotiations. Indeed, over many years, we tried again and again to achieve this result to no avail. The Commonwealth Group of Eminent Persons has now added its confirmation that the Botha regime is not prepared to resolve the problems of South Africa by negotiations. It is instead as committed as ever to maintain the system of White minority rule by repression and violence.

This surely must lay to rest the illusion that negotiations are an option available to us and confirm the hollowness and bankruptcy of arguments that decisive action should be avoided in the interests of promoting the chances of a negotiated settlement. The call made on us to renounce violence, as it is put, is nothing but a ruse to render us impotent precisely for the purpose of ensuring the perpetuation of the apartheid system. We shall certainly not fall into that trap.

It is significant who is making this call. It is those, who are wielding power and armed force against the people. They who are shooting our people down will come to the conference table armed. But we must go there empty-handed!

To achieve change, we must and will continue to intensify our political and military offensive. We owe it to ourselves as a people and to the thousands who have died. We owe it to the peoples of Southern Africa, the peoples of Africa and the rest of the world. We, as the representatives within South Africa, believing in the objectives contained in the Charter of the United Nations and the Declaration of Human Rights, count on you all to give us all-round support. The obligation to choose, to be on the side of the oppressed people of our country and their national liberation movement can no longer be avoided.

APARTHEID CANNOT BE REFORMED

Extract from the address by Oliver Tambo to the International Labour Organisation, Geneva, June 19, 1986.

Our struggle has entered a phase, which marks the final days of the apartheid system of colonial and racist domination. The extraordinary challenge represented by the mass offensive, which has gripped our country over the last two years especially has as its point of focus the objectives of the transfer of power to the people.

It is centred on the urgent necessity for all South Africans to govern our country together, to determine its future as equals, to fashion it into a peaceful and prosperous motherland, the common patrimony of all its people, both Black and White.

Thus, the struggle does not seek what the Botha regime describes as reforms. It is not about partial improvements in the conditions of life of the Black oppressed majority. And of cardinal importance in this regard is the fact that the idea has taken root in the minds of the millions of our people that if we must perish, as some of us will, then we will lay down our lives not for peripheral changes but for a genuine social and political transformation of our reality. Of equal importance is the awareness that we have it in our power to bring this new reality into being, that our daily sacrifices are necessary elements in the actual making of a glorious future.

The Pretoria regime is responding to this democratic challenge as we would expect it to. This regime remains committed to the maintenance of the apartheid system. In its essence, this system is about the monopolisation of political power by the White minority. Everything that the Botha regime does is

86

directed at ensuring that whatever happens the White minority retains political control for all time.

We consider it a matter of great importance that the international community should understand this fully and clearly. This is especially necessary at a time when the Botha regime projects itself as reformist and a new-found opponent of apartheid. This regime seeks to reduce world hostility to the apartheid system in order to weaken the pressure for sanctions and buy a further lease of life for itself. Among the so-called reforms carried out by the Botha regime are the repeal of the racist sex and marriage laws, amendments to labour legislation and proposed changes affecting influx control and the pass laws. None of these addresses to the fundamental question of the urgent need to ensure that all the people of South Africa participate in governing our country. They do not in any way affect the future of power in our country.

As we have said so many times, apartheid cannot be reformed. It must be destroyed in its entirety. For, indeed, how do you reform oppression? How do you reform the domination of the Black majority by the White minority? How do you reform a crime so that it ceases to be a crime? Oppression and freedom are antithetical and mutually exclusive, they cannot be made to co-exist by the injection of the word 'reform'. Botha understands this.

Indeed, while talking of reforms, he has made it plain on many occasions that he will not depart from his objective of maintaining the system of White minority domination. He, therefore, speaks consistently of so-called group rights, of the right of the White population to self-determination and of South Africa being a nation of minorities, whose rights must be protected. All of these are mere euphemisms for apartheid, according to which the population must continue to be defined in racial and ethnic categories and subjected to domination by the White minority.

Far from being interested in change, the apartheid regime sees its principal task as the destruction of those forces that are fighting for a united, democratic and non-racial South Africa.

87

In this regard, Pretoria is also involved in feverish activities to expand its machinery of repression and continuously escalates the use of force and terror against the people. To justify all this, the racists have elaborated and advanced the so-called doctrine of national security, according to which everything the regime does must serve to reinforce the safety of the apartheid system.

In practice, not only is the Botha regime continuously expanding its armed forces, but it has also ensured that these forces occupy a critical place in its governing structures. Twice in a period of less than a year, States of Emergency have been declared during which the army and the police have been given powers of life and death over millions of our people. This is the situation in South Africa today. It is one of rule by the gun.

The pre-eminence of the option of state terrorism in the response of the Pretoria regime to the heightened struggle in our country should of course, come as no surprise. After all, apartheid is violence. The establishment of a social system, in which a section of the population is defined as the underling and another as the master is itself an act of violence — an act of violence, which can only acquire permanence by the continuing use of violence. It is, therefore, logical that such a system should respond to any crisis not only with an increased use of force, but also with the glorification of violence as a cult and a necessary means of ordering social relations.

The Botha, who is today promoted by some in certain Western countries as the most reform-minded head of state that racist South Africa has ever had, in fact, epitomises this cult of violence and is proud to consider himself a skilled practitioner in the use of force to achieve political objectives.

The same considerations about the role of violence stand at the centre of the policy of the Pretoria regime vis-a-vis the independent States of our region. Over the years, Pretoria has advanced various theses to justify its campaign of aggression against these States. The most current of these is the assertion by the Pretoria regime that apartheid South Africa has a natural role as a regional power.

88

In advancing this claim, Pretoria once more moves from the proposition that force is the principal determinant of the structure of inter-state relations. From this flows ineluctably the idea of spheres of influence, the idea of a natural and organic international periphery, whose extent and adherence to the centre are determined by the strength of that centre and the skill with which the centre uses its power to assert its influence.

The assertion made by the Botha regime after its recent raids into Botswana, Zambia and Zimbabwe that its actions were no different from those carried out by the Reagan Administration against Libya was consistent with its view of the role of force in the ordering of international relations. The Pretoria regime sees its position in relation to Southern Africa and Africa as a whole as no different from that of the United States with regard to the Caribbean and Central and South America.

The meaning of all this for Southern Africa is quite clear. It is that while it has the capacity to do so, the apartheid regime will continue in its efforts to dominate the region, through aggression, destabilisation and subversion. Even in the inevitable situation, when the escalation of the struggle for national liberation inside South Africa will have stretched the enemy forces to their limit, we must still expect that the Pretoria regime will continue to hit out at our neighbours. Indeed, the logic of its position would demand of the Pretoria regime that in such a situation, aggressive forays should be both swift and very destructive.

The apartheid regime upholds and will continue to assume this posture because, in terms of its own calculations, it has permanent tasks to keep the neighbouring states economically and politically unstable and to ensure that they do not become active supporters of the ANC.

There are, therefore, various elements that are inherent in the strategy of survival of the South African regime, including complete rejection of international norms concerning independence of states and the inviolability of their borders and sovereignty. This strategy also assumes a definition of international peace and security, which hinges on the thesis that the strong are entitled to violate such peace and security to enable them to establish a stable order based on the subservience of the weak to the will of the strong.

In its report, the Commonwealth Group of Eminent Persons has warned of the certainty of unspeakable bloodshed in Southern Africa if the international community does not intervene by imposing effective sanctions. It should be clear from what we have said that we ourselves agree with this conclusion. The use of violence is an imperative, internal to the apartheid system, inherent in it, the motor that drives its engine of survival. Already a man-hating system, apartheid will be particularly destructive to the Black people because, in any case, it describes us as less than human and, therefore, capable of being annihilated as so much vermin.

But our people are moved by the same desires and impulses that have motivated men and women through the ages to assert their right to liberty. Our very humanity impels us to act boldly and consistently to end a man-made system, whose basic philosophy is the degradation, dehumanisation and immolation of an entire people. Contrary to the wishes of the rulers, the more violence they use, the greater the determination of the victims of that violence to end the situation of terror. And yet, the more people resist, the more the oppressor believes that all that is wrong is that he has not used sufficient force.

In the struggles that are raging in our country today, and which have persisted without a day's respite for so long, our people are showing that the might of the cause of justice can never be dwarfed or denied by the terror of guns and evil state power. In the streets of our towns and cities and in the villages, in direct daily confrontation with the enemy army and police, the millions of the unarmed are moving forward steadily in the struggle towards the realisation of the objective we have set ourselves — to destroy the apartheid system and create a democratic and non-racial society in its place.

Our movement and our people have had their own flag and national anthem for well over half a century now. This came about simply because, when Britain handed over power exclusively to the White minority in 1910, leaving our colonial status unchanged, we refused to recognise the then Union of South Africa and its symbols of state as our own.

The struggle we have waged since then has resulted in the emergence in South Africa today of the democratic movement as the alternative power. The desperate acts of the apartheid regime derive from its realisation that our movement for national liberation is challenging the very existence of the apartheid state. Today, that movement is recognised by the overwhelming majority of our people as their authentic representative, their political leader. The recent successful general strike called to observe the tenth anniversary of the Soweto Uprising of June 16, 1976 was held despite the proclamation of a State of Emergency, the arrest of many leaders and activists and the deployment of the army and police in massive numbers throughout the country. This clearly demonstrated the authority, which the movement enjoys among our people.

Our programme, the Freedom Charter, is the property of the people, uniting them in their millions as their perspective for the kind of South Africa we are fighting for.

On the other hand, the apartheid system is immersed in a deep and worsening economic, political and social crisis from which it cannot extricate itself. The apartheid regime has been thrown into disarray. At the same time, the White power bloc is rent by divisions and conflict and can never regain even a semblance of unity and common purpose.

All this has come about because of the intensity and the consistency of the all-round political and military struggle that continues to escalate in both South Africa and Namibia, complemented and reinforced by the international offensive to isolate the Pretoria regime. The task that faces us is to step up this struggle to even higher levels in a combined political and military offensive.

IMPOSE COMPREHENSIVE MANDATORY SANCTIONS

Address by the ANC President, Oliver Tambo, to the Royal Commonwealth Society, London, June 23, 1986.

Exactly eight months ago to the day, in Nassau, the capital of the Bahamas, the Heads of States and Governments of the Commonwealth countries assembled to debate the South African issue, strictly from the point of view of what the Commonwealth wanted to do to bring about an end to the apartheid system. The question was whether sanctions or no sanctions. Part of the reason why we are gathered here today is that that question has not yet been resolved. We meet to address the same question that the Commonwealth faced in the Bahamas. The invitation to us to address you on this occasion, which we greatly appreciate, and your presence, demonstrate the profound interest and concern of the Royal Commonwealth Society over developments in Southern Africa.

It would seem to us clear that in the recent past, a good deal of progress has been made towards the clarification of various issues. This relates not only to the issue of what should be done to end apartheid, but also the question of what should take its place. The current international debate hinges, therefore, on the question of how to make this country, Britain, take its proper position among the countries of the Commonwealth and the majority of the international community of nations.

As we know, in its recalcitrance, Britain is not alone. The problem of how to act effectively on the South African situation boils down to the question of how to win, how to compel the support of the United States, Great Britain and the Federal Republic of Germany for the cause of the victims of apartheid. The positions that these countries take are supportive of a crime against humanity, the permanence of White minority domination over the Black majority.

Recently, the debate has come to concentrate on the question of the effectiveness of measures to be imposed upon Pretoria in order to bring about as peaceful a resolution of that country's problems as possible. Questions are being raised about the effectiveness of economic measures, the possibility of their adoption universally, their impact on a liberated, post-apartheid South Africa, their effect on the independent sovereign states of Southern Africa and related issues. All these questions are part of the on-going debate.

But there are pointers, very clear pointers, to the direction that this debate is taking. I have referred to Nassau, the striking unanimity of the Commonwealth countries, save for the position of Britain. From Nassau came the Commonwealth Group of Eminent Persons. They were directed to examine that situation and see whether the Pretoria regime was ready to behave in such a way as to make it unnecessary, perhaps, to consider sanctions. The Eminent Persons have passed their judgment and it is in the hands of the international public.

Twice in the recent past, the UN Security Council has met, again to consider action arising out of developments in Southern Africa. Twice, resolutions intended to see the international community take action, were defeated by the veto exercised against those resolutions by the United States and Britain.

Last week, a World Conference to discuss sanctions against South Africa met in Paris, attended by many countries of the world, with delegations led by Foreign Ministers. That Conference came to the conclusion that the demand of the situation in South Africa on those, who want to see a resolution of that problem is sanctions.

And we think it is important that as we debate these questions, we should never forget that there is a horrendous situation in which violence is being perpetrated against millions of our people everyday — as a matter of course. We refer here not only to the daily shootings, the bestialities inflicted on demonstrators and detainees and the vicious campaign of terror carried out against all who are opposed to the apartheid system — churchmen, whole religious communities, students, professors and teachers, workers, peasants, mothers and even children. No one is excepted.

Nor is this the end. It is certainly not the beginning. This is the situation we have endured since the beginning of the apartheid era. It simply gets worse and worse. Thousands, hundreds of thousands of people have perished under the apartheid system, and because of it. The suffering has been massive and it worsens day by day. The imposition of a State of Emergency is evidence of a worsening situation.

And so in a sense the international community does not have the leisure to be taking its own time, debating inconsequential issues such as the fact that action in the form of sanctions will affect all the people of South Africa, including the victims of the apartheid system.

It is idle, in the face of the destruction in terms of life which the apartheid system has caused, to be saying nothing should be done, because the Blacks will suffer. That kind of argument displays lack of knowledge, lack of appreciation of what apartheid has been and continues to be. It is the pain of apartheid that we want to stop by ending apartheid. We are not asking for pity for our suffering. We are asking to be supported for the sacrifices we are ready to make and are making. The burdens that sanctions will bring upon us are a sacrifice we are prepared to make.

The deaths that we suffer in the course of struggle is a sacrifice, we are ready to make. We ask for no pity. We ask for support from those who, we believe, in our position would feel compelled to do what we are doing to seek to end the pain of apartheid.

It should also be remembered that as long as the apartheid

system and the apartheid regime feel free to take their own time over what should be done, for so long shall we wait, before those of our people, who have been consigned to prison for more than two decades, shall be released. Outstanding leaders of our people and many others are being held this minute as caged animals simply because they dared to demand the liberty of our people. They were caged, Mr. Chairman, when I came into this hall. This minute they are still there.

To their credit, their morale is as high as it ever was before, because they continue to have faith that the international community is on their side, not simply by way of declarations, but by using its great potential to change the fortunes of the apartheid system in favour of the majority of the people of South Africa and Southern Africa as well.

We speak also of the inhuman burden imposed on millions of our people, who have been banished to the Bantustans, the countless numbers of children, who die from sheer hunger, the tens of thousands of Crossroads and others like them who are being forcibly uprooted and literally shot and butchered to compel them to live elsewhere to satisfy the apartheid designs of the Botha regime. When we talk about sanctions, we are addressing the current, ongoing misery that these people must bear.

In addressing the question 'What is to be done', it should be borne in mind that as each day passes and no action is taken, so an extra day is added in the perpetuation of this crime against humanity. Those who refuse to act accordingly make the resolution of the South African problem more complicated. But because our people are not sitting passively, but are suffering bravely, they are challenging the apartheid monster. They are seeking to do and achieve what the international community would want to see - an end to the crime against humanity.

There is no need for us here to go over the ground that has so brilliantly been covered by the Commonwealth Group of Eminent Persons. It should suffice that we emphasise only some of its conclusions. These are that the Botha regime is

95

determined to maintain the apartheid system of White minority domination by force; that its so-called reforms constitute an attempt to strengthen this system, that violence against the people is an inherent feature of this system, and that the firm belief that the leading Western powers will not impose sanctions has encouraged the Botha regime to pursue its apartheid policy regardless of its complete rejection by our people and the rest of the international community.

The Group of Eminent Persons has also recognised the fact that, in the light of all this, we have no alternative but to fight and has correctly warned of an impending catastrophe of immense dimensions. To avoid that eventuality, the EPG has called on the Commonwealth, and indeed the rest of the world, to impose effective economic measures, which means sanctions against apartheid South Africa.

One of the most pressing questions that arises from all this is what the British government should do in response to this Report, to the situation which obtains in South Africa and to the demands of the public, both here and abroad. We believe that the British government can no longer shirk its responsibilities to act decisively in support of the democratic anti-racist forces of our country. The fact that this country also has the honour to be one of the permanent members of the Security Council imposes on its government an obligation to act for justice and peace in South and Southern Africa.

Failure to do so not only lowers the prestige of the Security Council but also puts in question the usefulness to the world community of the institution itself. It surely cannot help to strengthen the Commonwealth, of which the people of this country are justly proud, that one of its leading members, the United Kingdom, should treat its collective view with contempt.

What we are calling for, and have been urging for decades, are comprehensive and mandatory sanctions now. We are convinced, advisedly, that a long drawn-out conflict in South Africa will most certainly result in the destruction of the economy, to say nothing of the scale of deaths of which the EPG and leaders of the Commonwealth such as President Kaunda have so repeatedly warned.

The argument for selective and incremental sanctions is flawed exactly because it perpetuates Pretoria's belief that this country and South Africa's other trading partners will only act merely to defuse pressures for meaningful action. It is also an argument for imposing sanctions in such a manner that South Africa should be permitted the possibility to adjust and to weather the consequences of each specific action.

Take, for instance, the call for a ban on new investment. The fact of the matter is that new investment in South Africa has all but dried up because of the obvious crisis in the country and the related parlous state of the economy. Simply to impose such a selective measure would be to send a signal to the Botha regime that the British government is still resolved not to act in any serious way.

The argument for comprehensive and mandatory sanctions is, of course, that such a massive blow would make it almost impossible for the apartheid regime to continue in power for much longer. Such comprehensive measures would naturally include financial and trade sanctions, an oil embargo, the termination of air and maritime links, ceasing of all co-operation in the nuclear field and the closing of all loopholes with regard to the embargo on arms and other materials related to the military capacity and the repressive state machinery of the Pretoria regime, as well as other measures within the sphere of comprehensive sanctions.

It will certainly be argued by some that we are being exceedingly unreasonable to make such a call. This we can only reiterate the point that the alternative to all this is that we will be left with nothing, but the inevitable choice to fight it out with everything we have. Indeed, we will always be doing this. The consequences of this are, as was once said, too ghastly to contemplate.

And yet, the prospect of something too ghastly to contemplate can be no deterrent to a people who are determined to have their freedom. It is not the power of the apartheid machinery or even its efficiency, that is the determining factor. It is our humanity. It is the fact that we are people, we are human. We have decided to liberate our country and ourselves, to get rid of a crime against us and humanity. We will make all the necessary sacrifices to achieve that end.

Those who equivocate on the question of economic sanctions, are preparing conditions, which will ensure that what most people would want to avoid does in fact occur. It has been called a 'bloodbath' and 'the reduction of South Africa to a wasteland'. Prospects of a bloodbath and the reduction of South Africa to a wasteland will not stop this struggle. We would much rather that no blood was lost, that the country was left intact. But not at the expense of our continued enslavement. It is in the hands of the international community, perhaps, today I should say in the hands of the Commonwealth, especially the Head of the Commonwealth to intervene on our side, on the side of humanity.

In the light of this, it will not do to persist with arguments that the Black people and the neighbouring states will suffer from the imposition of sanctions. We have dealt with that. The key factor is that in the absence of sanctions, the conflict with all its consequences will multiply itself a hundredfold, and more. We believe also that the time has come for an end to the interminable debate about the effectiveness or non-effectiveness of sanctions.

Practice itself has answered this question. To add to this, the Pretoria regime has admitted publicly how much it fears sanctions, exactly because of their effectiveness. According to the Proclamation declaring a State of Emergency earlier this month, it is on offence to 'encourage or promote disinvestment or the application of sanctions or foreign action against the Republic.' If sanctions were of no consequence and would have no effect, it would not have been necessary for Pretoria to adopt such a position.

We are at war against the ap rtheid system and its inhumanities, for the right to be human in a land of humans. We, therefore, are determined to fight alone if necessary. In that sense, we view sanctions as a complementary form of action to the struggle we are waging, and must intensify, within the country. We do not see sanctions by themselves as ending the apartheid system. We see them as aiding the speedy end of the apartheid system.

An important element in that struggle is the mobilisation of all our people, including our White compatriots, to act against the apartheid regime. The argument that sanctions would drive the Whites into a *laager* fails to take into account the fact that many Whites are in fact joining this struggle. We are convinced that as the price for maintaining the apartheid system rises, so will it be clear to many more of these White South Africans that the time for change has come.

We are convinced that a consensus in favour of sanctions has emerged in this country. We are encouraged by the positions that various sections of the British public have taken, including some among the business community. We are convinced that given the political will, there exists today the possibility to oblige the British government to act in a meaningful way.

At the same time, there still exists a great reservoir of opinion in this country which cannot be described in any other way than racist, I am afraid. This was reflected in a newspaper yesterday which made bold to state that "African Blacks, inside and outside the Republic, (are) for the most part so backward." 'African Black' means the Black people in Africa. Some, of course, are in Africa. They are all "backward." And the point that is being made in the article is that the international community tends to forget the factor of race—they are "backward" because they are Black. The writer concludes that they are backward and "White supremacy (in South Africa) is there to stay."

These comments are made in the context of explaining the positions of the British Prime Minister in opposing sanctions and suggests that she appreciates this fact of "backwardness." But the writer also believes—we submit wrongly, we wait to be proved wrong—that the majority of the British public are also aware of this "backwardness" and, therefore, the permanence of White supremacy in South Africa. And if that is the position, who would want to oppose White supremacy, if it is going to be there forever? This is given in explanation of the position of the British government. It is an opinion credited to the British public.

If the Commonwealth breaks up because of the intransigence of the British Government, it would be an unfortunate but inevitable conclusion that those who have the power to decide will have been influenced by such racist notions as were reflected in the newspaper to which we have referred. The impression we have that the British Government considers as not very important the views of the Commonwealth as opposed to those of its NATO and EEC allies, emphasis the need for the British government to act correctly if it is not to be seen to be contributing to the exacerbation of world racial tensions.

And we trust that the countries of the Commonwealth will not allow themselves to be dragged into an alliance against the people of Africa, however "backward" they may be, into an alliance against the people of Southern Africa, into an alliance with apartheid. The time calls for great firmness.

We have, in the past, said that the unconditional release of all political prisoners is a pre-requisite to any consideration on our part of a negotiated settlement of the South African question. Nothing has happened in this regard except a continuing and stubborn insistence by the Botha regime that these leaders, as well as the ANC as such, must renounce violence — and this in a situation in which the most massive violence against our people is being perpetrated every day, violence which is being hidden behind the most comprehensive news blackout that our country has ever seen.

We are convinced, as the EPG was, that the Botha regime is not ready for negotiations. Nevertheless, we remain of the view that the campaign for the immediate and unconditional release of all political prisoners must continue to build up to even higher levels of intensity.

Surely, it should be obvious to everybody that once these patriots are released unconditionally and the situation thus created for all our leaders, across the entire spectrum of the

100

democratic movement, to come together and have the possibility of discussing the situation as it is today, and its demands, as well as the way forward, this would also provide the possibility for us to address even the question of negotiations as a leadership. Once this happens, we can then address the question of negotiations, on the basis that a demonstration has been made by the Botha regime of its seriousness about negotiations.

Those of us who have lived in Southern Africa over the past ten years have experienced the attitude of the Pretoria regime towards negotiations. The record is dismal. It has never negotiated anything seriously, not with the Mozambicans, not with the Angolans, not with the Namibians. We do not want a repetition of so-called "meaningful negotiations."

Pretoria must prove its bona fides. It is not possible to negotiate with someone you totally distrust in regard to his aims about negotiation. We will not participate in giving the Pretoria regime the possibility of extending its lease of life by pretending to be negotiating. But it can demonstrate its serious intention to negotiate. Its words do not add up to anything. It is its actions that must speak.

The next few weeks are very important to us because, by their concrete actions, the government of Great Britain, the rest of the EEC and the United States will demonstrate whether they are ready and willing to take sides against apartheid by imposing sanctions or whether they insist on continuing to underpin White minority rule which prevails in our country.

If the Botha regime, as it claims, has not used a tenth of its might against those who want to see a new order in South Africa — a non-racial, democratic and united South Africa — if they have not used one tenth of their might against us, then neither have we used a tenth of our strength. We count on all who are present here to act in support of our cause; to push the British government to join those who would want to stop the Botha regime from pushing South Africa over the brink.

RACISM, APARTHEID AND
A NEW WORLD ORDER

This is the full text of the Third World Lecture 1986
delivered by Oliver Reginald Tambo under the auspices of
the Third World Foundation 1986, in London. The Third
World Prize of the Foundation for that year was awarded
to Nelson and Winnie Mandela. Reproduced through
courtesy of the Third World Foundation, London.

The most senior leaders of the oppressed people of South
Africa have been in prison for almost a quarter of a century
now. They, who would have contributed so enormously to
the making of a prosperous, happy and peaceful society, whose
leadership would have moved millions to strive for the achievement of this goal, these have been condemned to commune
only with the prison guards for the rest of their natural lives.

While these titans of freedom pounded rocks and sewed mail-
bags behind prison walls, those who had issued the command
that they should be jailed were busy imprisoning a whole
society. They decreed that none shall speak of anything except
what the goalers permitted to be said; that one shall act according to their consciences except with the authorisation of the
gendarme. They proclaimed that the truth shall not be told
except that which the regime of repression deemed to be the
truth. They, on the other hand, would have the right to
designate oppression as liberty; those who are enslaved would
be described as free men and women, while he or she that dared
to fight for genuine freedom would be categorised and treated
as a criminal.

We are meeting here today to honour two South Africans,

Nelson and Winnie Mandela, who symbolise those prisoners, the first within the narrower and the second, the wider meaning of that term. We meet not to express sympathy either with them or with the millions of people of whom they a are part, but rather, to salute and pay tribute to them for their resistance to tyranny. We have gathered here to honour them for their steadfastness in the struggle to give birth to a world in which those of us, who are blessed with the skin colour you see on our hands and faces, will no longer be victims of oppression, exploitation and degradation.

The cause for which our people are paying the supreme sacrifice daily and for which Nelson Mandela, Walter Sisulu, Govan Mbeki, Harry Gwala, Ahmed Kathrada, Elias Motsoaledi and others have been sentenced to life imprisonment, has a significance which extends far beyond the borders of our country.

For, what they are fighting against is the pernicious ideology of racism, the accumulated refuse of centuries of an anti-human prejudice, which seeks to define people as inferior, as not fully human, by virtue of their race. They are engaged in the struggle to end the practice, which gave birth to these ideas, the practice of racial discrimination, racial oppression, domination and exploitation.

Racisim, one of the great evils of our time, bedevils human relations, between individuals, within and between nations and across continents. It brutalises entire peoples, destroys persons, warps the process of thought and injects into human society a foul air of tension, mutual antagonism and hatred. It demeans and dehumanises both victim and practitioner, locking them into the vile relationship of master race and *untermenschen*, superior and underling, each with his position defined by race.

As Black South Africans, we have lived within the entrails of the racist beast for many a long year. We have seen constructed a system of social organisation based on the premise and the practice that those, who are White are inherently superior and those who are Black must, in their own interests, be the objects of policies decided exclusively and solely by the White people.

Quite clearly, this edifice required some pseudo-theoretical percepts to underpin it and give it the appearance of rationality. The theoreticians of racism in our country drew on the gross perversions of science, which assumed their clearest forms during the second half of the last century in Europe and the United States. In these centres of imperialist power, there grew up theories that biology and social anthropology provided the basis to justify the notion that all Black people carried with them both an innate and a cultural inferiority to the White, giving the latter the right and the duty of guardianship over the former.

Implicit in this thesis is the idea that these higher human beings have a similar right and duty to maintain the purity of the human species upto the point and including the commission of the crime of genocide.

One of the earliest of these racist theoreticians in our country, this century, was none other than General Jan Smuts, who opposed Nazism only because it threatened British imperial power. Speaking amidst the splendour of the London Savoy Hotel in 1917, Smuts had this to say:

"It has now become an accepted axiom in our dealings with the natives that it is dishonourable to mix White and Black blood... We have felt more and more that if we are to solve our native question, it is useless to try to govern Black and White in the same system, to subject them to the same institutions of government and legislation. They are different not only in colour but in minds and in political capacity ..." (Quoted in: Wilkins and Strydom: *The Broederbond*; Paddington Press Ltd, London 1979.)

More than 40 years later, when these insulting racist ideas had been translated into the apartheid system, here is what two other theoreticians of this system wrote:

"The three foundation stones of apartheid are Western culture, Christian morality and a specific racial identity. In the case of

104

the Afrikaner, there is a powerful connecting link between these three elements. His own particular bio-genetic character is, for example, associated with a particular socio-cultural way of life and to give up either, through amalgamation with a more primitive culture or race must necessarily result in the destruction of the other." (Quoted in: Pierre van den Berghe: *South Africa — a Study in Conflict*, University of California Press, Berkeley, 1967 quoting N.J. Rhoodie and H.J. Venter.)

Of course, the inanities that were being conveyed as biogenetic and socio-cultural theory, during the second halves of both the 19th and the 20th centuries, were nothing but an attempt to justify a colonial reationship of the domination and exploitation of the Black peoples by the Whites. They had absolutely nothing to do with scientific truth.

Once implanted and despite their exposure as fraudulent and bankrupt, these ideas seemed to take on an independent existence, nurtured by the continued practice of White supremacy in many parts of the globe. Originating from practice, they served to encourage the entrenchment, perpetuation and extension of this practice. To emphasise the point that they reflected an immutable natural order of things, the fertile human mind goes further to enrobe these racist ideas and practices with the cloak of religion.

It is indeed in this way that it becomes possible for racism to give those who believe themselves to be superior, the power to challenge the very God they dragoon to serve their interests and whom they claim to worship. Thus, whereas the Christian scriptures, for instance, see all human beings as having been created in God's image, all racists will, for reasons that are perfectly obvious to them, retort that this cannot be so. And so it is that the foulest of crimes, against life itself, are perpetrated in the name of religion, as it the case in our own country to the earlier missionaries, derived exactly from this view that the European was a higher being deposited on this planet to play God over "the natives."

From what we have said so far, it is self-evident that the practical relationship that characterised the interaction between

Europe and the colonised world, today's Third World, could not be but a hothouse of ideas justifying this relationship. In its essence, racism is therefore about domination and works both to justify existing domination and to prescribe domination as the *sine qua non* for the solution of all future problems.

Among the objectives pursued by our illustrious host here today, the Third World Foundation, are "to assist in the evolution of a fundamentally just and equitable relationship between the Third World and the developed countries" as well as "to create greater awareness of the problems of poverty, hunger and ignorance in the Third World."

That it is necessary to address to these issues, as indeed it is, attests to the fact that the imbalance of strength, the inequality of power and the incompatibility of objectives that marked the relations between the imperialist powers and the colonised peoples remain to this day. It is not necessary for us to elaborate further on this to those who are gathered here and have to contend with its disastrous consequences daily.

The point we must, however, emphasise is that it is exactly in these conditions that racism thrives, as it did during the colonial period. Hence, we still find current notions that at the base of the "North-South" dichotomy, lies the difference between the White peoples in the North, who are inventive, industrious and disciplined and the Blacks in the South, who are innately indolent, imitative and happy-go-lucky.

Western Europe has large numbers of so-called *gastarbeiter*, who are mainly non-European workers from the South. The jobs they do, the squalor in which many of them live, the ghettoes in which they are concentrated, once more emphasise the distinction between Black and White as well as the lowly position of the former and the superiority and domination of the latter.

Similarly, in the United States, one has only to see the statistics of unemployment, drug addiction, homelessness, single-parent families and so on, to realise the extent to which the Black population is marginalised and serves as a living example for the most backward elements to "prove" the assertion that to be Black is to belong to a category of the human species that is less than human and which must be used as befits its status.

All of us present here know that the causes that account for the relationship between Black and White, and North and South, that we have been talking about, are neither biogenetic nor socio-cultural. Rather, they are socio-economic and are therefore capable of being changed or removed. Indeed, it is the resolve to bring about a fundamentally just and equitable relationship between the Third World and the developed countries' that led to the emergence of such important groupings as the Non-Aligned Movement and the Group of 77.

Those who are interested in an end to racism must necessarily be concerned that these organisations should succeed. In as much as the huge nuclear arms expenditures are incompatible with development, so is the growing relative and absolute underdevelopment of millions upon millions of Black people incompatible with the objective of ridding the world of racial arrogance, discrimination and tyranny.

The urgent need for a New International Economic Order has been dramatically illustrated by the famine in Africa, the international debt crisis and the collapse of the price of oil and other raw materials. The hard and continuing struggle for the New Order is fundamentally about the re-distribution of the world means of production, to bring about the economic independence of the Third World and enable its peoples to banish hunger, disease and ignorance for ever, to assert their dignity as human beings and bring fulfilment to their lives. The accomplishment of this objective would itself redress the political imbalance which threatens the independence of many nations, thanks to the extension of the infamous Monroe Doctrine by the present US Administration to cover the entire Third World.

We, the peoples, who were objects of imperialist expansionism, forever the infantile dwarfs, who required the benign or brutal patronage of the White "Superman", in earlier times had to be liberated from the state of noble savagery. Whether this resulted in our transportation across the seas as slaves or in enslavement in our own countries, as subject peoples, was but the unfolding of the manifest destiny.

Today, still the infantile dwarfs as of yore, unable to think for ourselves, inanimate fruit ready for the picking by whosoever has sufficient strength to rule the garden patch, we are being taken under the protective wing of the United States, to save us from falling victim to an alleged Communist expansionism.

Angola and Mazombique, Nicaragua and Libya, Grenada, El Salvador and Namibia are the victims of this eminently racist policy, which asserts the supremacy of the interests of the United States over those of the peoples of the Third World, which presumes, as General Smuts put it, that we have neither the minds nor the political capacity to exercise the right to self-determination.

It is clear that the fate that has befallen these countries will be visited on even more of us. Over the last few years, we have seen a discernible swing to the Right in all the major Western countries, with the dominant social groups infusing public consciousness with the notion that might is right. And, in good measure, we have seen the exercise of the White might against the Black people, be it in street brawls in British or French towns or in the invasion of countries.

Apartheid in South Africa exists as the concentrated expression of the world-wide cancer of racism that we have been talking about. In our country, the ideas and practices of racism reign supreme, as they did in Nazi Germany — the essence and the purpose of state policy, the instrument to effect and guarantee the domination and exploitation of the Black majority by the White minority.

Because of its high pedigree in reactionary political thought and praxis throughout the world, the apartheid system serves also as the nursery for the cultivation and propagation of the same man-hating policies, which the United Nations Organisation was formed to stamp out. It is because there is today widespread recognition of this reality that there exists that important instrument of international law — the Convention for the Suppression and Punishment of the Crime of Apartheid, which defines apartheid as a crime against humanity.

We assert it as an incontrovertible truth that mankind is under an obligation to suppress and punish this crime against humanity. On the basis of the experience of our own people of the horrendous practice of racism, we can categorically state it here that this crime cannot be suppressed by means of words or by persuading its perpetrators to desist from the commission of a crime.

Racism, the theory and practice of the domination of one race by another, and specifically its apartheid expression, cannot be reformed. Like Nazism, its antecedent and sister crime against humanity, it must be overthrown and uprooted forcibly, in its totality. Those who argue to the contrary and even claim that the Pretoria regime has embarked on reform, are either grossly misled or are bent on protecting the regime of racial tyranny by seeking to refurbish its image to make it more acceptable.

In any case, a cancer cannot be its own cure. The fanatical racists who have spent more than half-a-century drawing up the blue-prints of the apartheid system and transforming those theoretical constructions into the South African society we know today, cannot, at the same time, be the agents for the abolition of that system.

All they know and will ever know, it is need to maintain the system of White supremacy, and to maintain it by the use of all the violence that they can muster. Today, our people are dying in large numbers, murdered on the orders of Pretoria's army and police generals. The blood-letting continues without reserve because, after all, those that are being killed are, in the eyes of the generals, lesser beings, who can be disposed of without compunction, because they are less than human. Some Western governments are pleased to describe this as the maintenance of law and order!

The same mentality and objective of the defence of White minority domination, has instructed and continues to inform the attitude and policy of the Pretoria regime towards the Frontline and other independent countries of Southern Africa. Its regular forces as well as its armed puppet formations have wrought untold damage especially on the people of Angola and

Mozambique, with an enormous loss in human lives. Racism cannot accept any relationship between Black and White except that between servant and master. Southern Africa will know no peace until the apartheid regime in South Africa is defeated and the system it upholds destroyed.

When that day dawns, only then will the full horror of the genocide being carried out in the Bantustans become visible for all to see. Whereas the Nazis resorted to the gas chamber to annihilate peoples they considered superfluous and no better than vermin, the Pretoria regime has used the method of death by starvation to carry out its mission of purifying the human race. The destruction of a system that has as one of its cornerstones such deliberate mass murder, is surely long overdue.

Yet the reality of the perpetuation of racism in South Africa is that the apartheid regime is supported by the same forces, which during the last century, deemed that the perspectives held out by the French and the American Revolutions were not for the colonised. The dominant forces in the major Western countries do this not despite the system of apartheid, but because of it.

They support racism because it expresses the imperative of the systems they represent, namely, to dominate, and serves their purposes as an instrument for the extreme exploitation of those who are dominated. For these reasons, they spurn our appeals for comprehensive sanctions against apartheid in South Africa, which we repeat today and urge upon the world community as the most effective means to bring about change in our country with the minimum of violence and destruction.

It was not a slip of the tongue but a frank admission of the truth when Ronald Reagan characterised the apartheid regime as an ally of long standing. His policy of constructive engagement with apartheid represents an engagement with racism that arises from the nature of imperialism — an engagement which, in the context of his goal to dominate the Third World, is constructive because it helps to strengthen the allied apartheid regime.

True to character, the Reagan Administration and others in

110

the West, make certain whenever they address the question of negotiations to resolve the conflict in our country, that they put the supposed interests and aspirations of the White minority first. They turn their own national experience of political change on their heads in order to serve the cause of racism in South Africa.

For example, it is argued forcefully that it is inappropriate and unreasonable for us to demand that all South Africans, both Black and White, should have an equal right to elect the government of their choice — in other words, to have a system of one-person-one-vote in a unitary state. Similarly, it is argued that it is we, the victims of the violence inherent in the apartheid system, we, who have to bury murdered children every day, who must lay down arms and cease our armed struggle to make negotiations possible. Countries, which are proud of the armed revolutions, which brought their peoples democracy are, because of their support for the racists, equally fervent in their denunciation of our armed combatants as terrorists.

Likewise, we must renounce all claims to the national wealth of our country, which we have created with our labour, because, by some queer logic, to say that the wealth of the country must be shared by all the people is, in the South African context, to threaten the human rights of the White minority.

From Washington, London, Bonn and Paris issues the call that it will be absolutely vital to safeguard the rights of the White minority. And yet from all these, which pride themselves as the centres of democracy, there is never a word about the rights of the majority — the non-racial majority! Instead, these centres of democracy are engaged in a desperate bid to find flunkeys and collaborators from among the Black people, who will be imposed on us as our true representatives and paid for their services, in order to preserve White privilege.

But certainly, no amount of political manoeuvring or killing of our people will blunt or stop the offensive of our masses, under the leadership of the African National Congress, to destroy racism in our country. Already the realisation is abroad among our people that victory is in sight.

It is a victory that we will use to build a truly democratic South Africa, one in which we shall abolish racism once and for all, and end the unjust and unequal relations of domination and exploitation that exist between Black and White in our country today and which are expressed in the concept and the practice of apartheid.

By that means, we shall also make our contribution to the struggle for a just and equitable international political, economic and social order and add as much as we can to the construction of a new world, free from racial discrimination and oppression, free from hunger and poverty and free from the threat of the termination of life itself through the use of nuclear weapons in a Third World War.

We count ourselves fortunate that we have among our people such outstanding humanists as Nelson and Winnie Mandela, as well as others such as Albertina Sisulu, Greta Ncapai, Dorothy Nyembe, Thandi Modise, Frances Baard, Vesta Smith, Amanda Kwadi, Barbara Hogan and Marion Sparg, people who hate racism and love all humanity enough to be prepared to die in the defence of liberty of all persons, regardless of their colour or race.

We are proud that we come of a people that, like all others, is not prepared to tolerate evil and acquiesce in the perpetuation of tyranny. In their names, we are happy to receive this eminent prize. We thank the Third World Foundation and all who are associated with it for having so honoured us. This prize will serve as a further spur for us and, we are certain, for the rest of humanity, to redouble our efforts to free all the political prisoners in our country and to liberate the millions of our people who are held hostage by a racist clique.

SOUTH AFRICA AT THE CROSSROADS

It was a befitting tribute to Oliver Tambo, when he was invited to deliver the 1987 Canon Collins Memorial Lecture on May 28, 1987, at London. Nothing could have pleased Canon Collins more, had he been alive. The following is the text of the lecture:

It is now almost five years since Canon John Collins passed away. With his departure, many of us lost a dear friend. As a people, we lost a fellow-combatant for justice and liberation, a dependable ally in the struggle to abolish the system of apartheid. Yet, such was the durability of his good works that it was inevitable that they would outlast the short life that is given to us all and thus serve to turn the memory of the man into a material force, that will continue to transform the destinies of the living.

As early as 1954, when he visited South Africa, he had the possibility not merely to study the situation as it then was, but more, to understand the nature of the apartheid system. From his assessment at the time, it was clear to him that South Africa, which he described as a 'madhouse', was heading for disaster. Even when some members of his own Church within South Africa denounced him for being a "foreign, meddling priest," Canon Collins did not waver in his involvement in the struggle against racist domination, precisely because he understood the dementia of this system.

We meet here today to pay a continuing tribute to him. Some of us have come here as his disciples. As such, all we can do is try to reflect on the message he left us, in the hope that we can communicate something of his example so that one or more

113

among us can be inspired to act as he did and thereby contribute their tithe to the banishment of evil.

Canon Collins came into our lives at the inception of the crisis which the imposition of the apartheid system was to bring to the people of South Africa. In 1952 and from 1955 onwards, he intervened in the persisting drama of South African politics to comfort the persecuted and to help save some of the most outstanding representatives of our people from possible death sentences or long terms of imprisonment. He came to our aid not in pity but in solidarity. He stretched out his hand to our people because he saw that what was happening to us was an unacceptable attack against humanity itself. He acted because he could not stand aside.

When the racist regime arrested and charged with high treason 156 leaders of our democratic movement in 1956, it hoped that it would destroy that movement and create a situation in which it would expand and entrench the apartheid system without opposition. John Collins took the side of those on trial, as he had supported the patriots who joined our Campaign in Defiance of Unjust Laws in 1952. His actions carried the message that in the struggle between the forces of democracy and those of racism, there can be no neutrality.

The crisis, which was in its early stages when Canon Collins joined us for the emancipation of our peoples, has matured. The septic boil caused by the apartheid system is ready to burst, as the brutally repressive casings, which contains the putrefaction of this system, ruptures irrevocably and for all time. South Africa is at the crossroads.

It has taken many years of struggle to reach the point at which we are today. In that period, tens of thousands have been killed, injured and imprisoned within South Africa. Thousands of others have suffered a similar fate in Namibia. The rest of Southern Africa has also seen enormous numbers of people die, economics forced to the verge of collapse and social programmes brought to halt.

Precisely that scale of destruction has only served to confirm the view among the victims of apartheid violence that they dare not give up, but have to fight with everything they can lay their hands on to end the system, that has brought about so much suffering. Above everything else, it is that resolve and determination by millions of people which guarantees the defeat of the Pretoria regime and the liquidation of the apartheid system.

And yet, there are those in this country who, unlike John Collins, doubt the certainty of our victory. They calculate that the racist regime is so powerful and the White minority so steadfast in its commitment to the maintenance of its domination that the oppressed are condemned to a futile and self-destructive battering at the ramparts of the racist fortress. But, of course, these Doubting Thomases also profess an abhorrence for apartheid and declare a desire to see it brought to an end.

These positions have resulted in a policy, which amounts to appeasement of the apartheid regime. Of central importance to the logical integrity of this policy is the notion that the Pretoria regime can and must be persuaded to turn itself into its opposite. Accordingly, it is required and expected that the racists should themselves dismantle the oppressive system they have instituted and over which they preside. Thus, would we see the miraculous conversion of oppressors into liberators and the consequent transformation of the liberation movement into an irrelevance.

Another important element in this equation is the definition of the essence of the policy that the White minority regime must follow, as repression and reform. In terms of this perspective, it is required that this regime should gradually reform the apartheid system out of existence. To do so, it is considered necessary that the supposed reformers should work their wonders in a situation of stability. Consequently, it is viewed as a *sine qua non* for the abolition of the apartheid system that the forces that are fighting against this system should be kept in check by repressive means.

It, therefore, seems clear to us that the major Western Powers have not departed from their old positions. According to them, the White minority regime is seen and treated as the defender and guarantor of the perceived interest of these powers. We, on the other hand, are viewed as a threat, which must be dealt with in the appropriate manner.

In response to all this, the questions might be posed — what of the fact that the governments of the principal Western powers have, especially during the last twelve months, entered into direct contact with the ANC? And what of the fact that these governments have repeatedly called on the Pretoria regime to enter into negotiations with everybody concerned, including the ANC?

The Western powers entered into official contact with the ANC because the argument that they were seeking change by talking exclusively to the Botha regime could no longer be sustained. It had lost credibility. In addition and as the Commonwealth Eminent Persons' Group understood and reported, it became clear to the Western governments that the majority of our people within South Africa recognised the ANC as their political representative. Hence, it was inevitable that, if they were still interested to project themselves as brokers, honest or otherwise, these governments would have to be seen to be talking to the ANC.

However, the decisions taken in the various capitals to relate to the ANC, did not in any way imply that there had been any change of attitude towards our policies, strategy and tactics. It is also obvious to us that in all the discussions we have held, by and large, we have failed to move such major Western powers as the USA, the United Kingdom and the Federal Republic of Germany to view the South African situation from the perspective of the oppressed.

On all major questions pertaining to the issues we are discussing, the coincidence of views between the Pretoria regime and the powers that be in most of the West persists. Where the racists describe us as a Communist front, Western governments go so far as to order secret investigation of the ANC to establish the extent of this alleged Communist domination.

Pretoria calls on us to renounce violence. The West calls on us to lay down arms. When the sole aggressor in Southern Africa

116

talks about so-called regional security, the Western Powers condemn "cross-border violence from all sides." The White minority regime conducts a vigorous campaign against sanctions and is joined in that campaign by the Western powers.

We can go on *ad infinitum* and speak even about the questions of formulations and terminology. For example, our armed struggle is never that, but is either terrorism or violence. The limpet mines we use are never simply limpet mines, but are either of Soviet or Communist origin. On the other hand, the guns and planes that Pretoria uses with such relish are never of British, American, French, Belgian or West German origin, but are mere guns or planes. The conclusions to draw from all this are obvious to all honest people.

It is true that repeated calls have been made on the Botha regime to enter into negotiations with its opponents. However, nothing is said about how this regime will ultimately be brought to the negotiating table. At the end of the day, the call for negotiations turns out to be nothing more than a pious wish. It is not a desire that is translated into policy, accompanied by the necessary measures to ensure that it succeeds as a policy.

With regard to the possibility for negotiations, the Commonwealth Eminent Persons' Group (EPG) observed correctly that "the attitude of the South African government was clearly going to be the single most important determining factor." At the end of their mission, the EPG concluded:

"It is our considered view that, despite appearances and statements to the contrary, the South African government is not yet ready to negotiate...(for the establishment of a non-racial and representative government) except on its own terms. Those terms, both in regard to objectives and modalities, fall far short of reasonable Black expectations and well-accepted democratic norms and principles."

Later on in its Report, the Group re-emphasised these points in the following manner:

"The government is in truth not yet prepared to negotiate fundamental change, nor to countenance the creation of genuine democratic structures, nor to face the prospect of the end of

White domination and White power in the foreseeable future. Its programme of reform does not end apartheid, but seeks to give it a less inhuman face. Its quest is power-sharing, but without surrendering overall White control."

Since the attitude of the Pretoria regime is the single most important factor determining the possibility for negotiations, and since that attitude is patently obvious, the test of the genuineness of the call for negotiations must necessarily turn on the willingness of those who make this call to change the attitude of the Pretoria regime towards these negotiations.

It is clear to us, as it was to the EPG and the Commonwealth mini-Summit to which the Group reported, that this cannot be done without pressure. As things stand, the Pretoria regime knows that it can continue to ignore the call for negotiations because the governments of the major Western countries have undertaken, almost as a matter of principle, that they will not act against the racist regime, despite its continued failure to respond to the universal demand for an end to the apartheid system and its replacement by a democratic social order.

It was obvious from the very beginning that Sir Geoffrey Howe's mission to South Africa, last year, would not succeed, precisely for the reason that both the British government and the EEC were committed to avoiding any effective sanctions against apartheid South Africa. The experiences of both the EPG and the British Foreign and Commonwealth Secretary underline the central point that what both we and the international community must focus our attention on is action to end the apartheid system. Everything, we do should be directed towards this end. We consider that any new international initiative seeking to bring about negotiations would be grossly misplaced and out of tune with reality exactly because the Botha regime is not prepared to address this fundamental question.

Nor indeed will it do to put the onus on the ANC to take such initiatives as it might be claimed would enable negotiations to take place; and neither will it do to fish around for such initiatives. If the key to negotiations were in our hands, we would long have used it to open the door. Such measures as have been proposed for us to adopt, namely, the cessation or suspension of our armed struggle or the unilateral proclamation of a moratorium will do nothing to bring about negotiations. The Pretoria regime is refusing to negotiate not because there is an armed struggle, but because it is unwilling to give up White minority domination. Once again, it is instructive to look at the observations of the Eminent Persons' Group on these issues. The EPG said:

"To ask the ANC or other parties, all of them far weaker than the government, to renounce violence for all time, here and now, would be to put them in a position of having to rely absolutely on the government's intentions and determination to press through the process of negotiations. It was not a question of whether the Group believed in the sincreity of the South African government, but whether the parties would. It was neither possible nor reasonable to have people forswear the only power available to them should the government walk away from the negotiating table. For the government to attribute all violence to the ANC ...was to overlook a situation in which the structures of society, dominated by a relatively small group of people, were founded upon injustice, which inevitably led to violence. In addition, in the light of recent events, the Government of South Africa would need to give a firm commitment to desist from further aggression against neighbouring states."

On the specific question of the suspension of armed struggle, the EPG stated that "a prior reduction in the level of violence before the government itself takes specific action in regard to the (Group's proposals) would not be feasible.... A suspension of violence or a commitment to non-violence, if in the government's view the meaning is the same, would obviously in the present context require a commitment to suspend the violence arising from the administration of apartheid."

Further, in one of its letters to the Pretoria regime the EPG makes the point that "the Lancaster House negotiations (on Zimbabwe) continued without the suspension of violence as have many others in situation of conflict." This is a matter of historical fact with which we are all familiar. It makes no sense that we should be treated as an exception to this general practice.

We also need to reiterate the point that the source of violence in South Africa, Namibia and our region is the apartheid system and the racist regime. What must cease is, in the words of the EPG, the violence that arises from the administration of apartheid. For that to happen, the system of White minority domination must be brought to an end. It seems to us strange reasoning that we, the victims of violence, should be asked to respond to the continued terror of the Pretoria regime against the peoples of Southern Africa by committing ourselves to cease our armed resistance, whether temporarily or permanently.

The Pretoria regime has blocked the path to negotiations. The recent Whites-only elections in South Africa have confirmed P.W. Botha in his view that White South Africa stands with him in his determination to resist all change and further to entrench the apartheid system. The governments of the Western countries that awaited the results of this illegitimate electoral process now have their answer. The question we would like to ask is what then are they going to do?

Those who have always been opposed to effective sanctions against racist South Africa are already advancing arguments to justify their old positions. These claim that White South Africa has moved further to the Right because of the sanctions that have been imposed. If it has not happened already, it will also be argued that the Botha regime has, as a result, become so strong that it will not be amenable to pressure—that all that can be done is to re-affirm the correctness of the policy of so-called constructive engagement.

All of this will, of course, come as music to the ears of the White supremacists in South Africa. Indeed, they will make certain that their friends state and re-state these arguments. We, on the other hand, are convinced that comprehensive and mandatory sanctions would succeed to break up this White power block by the maintenance of the apartheid system to a level that is unacceptable even for the most devoted adherents of this system. It is certainly our task to realise this objective and to achieve the transfer of power to the people through struggle.

We say that apartheid cannot be reformed but has to be abolished in its entirety. Official Western policy towards South Africa will not change until this correct proposition is accepted, until the example set by Canon Collins is adopted as the only legitimate course open to those, who say they want to see an end to apartheid.

This places the Western powers in the position in which they have to choose either to work for the total elimination of the apartheid system or, in fact, to connive at its perpetuation, as they do now. We are, however, certain that sooner or later they will come to realise that there has emerged an alternative democratic power within South Africa, an indigenous product of struggle, which holds the future of South Africa in its hands.

The West will then have to decide whether it takes the side of this alternative power and the rest of the anti-colonial and anti-racist forces of the continent of Africa made up of nearly 500 million people or whether it ties itself to the doomed course followed by far less than five million Africans of European origin. It is no longer possible to run with the hares and hunt with the hounds.

The alternative power in our country is as real today as it is impossible to vanquish in the future. It is here to stay and will grow in strength despite all efforts to suppress it, until South Africa is liberated and peace returns to Southern Africa. As a consequence of this development, it is becoming impossible to avoid confronting the question of the legitimacy of the powers, which are contending with each other within our country. These two cannot co-exist, as fascism and democracy could not, but have to give way one to the other.

Not even the best of conjurers can maintain an equidistant position between them. The times demand that you, who are gathered in this hall, should progress from opposition to apartheid to identification with and support for the democratic movement for national liberation in Namibia and South Africa. This evolution can no longer be avoided.

The broad perspectives of our country's democratic power are spelt out in the Freedom Charter. Organisationally it is represented by many formations, which recognise the leading role of the ANC in the struggle for a united, democratic and non-racial South Africa. Whether or not they support or engage in armed struggle, they are at one with us in seeking this outcome and are active in the struggle for its realisation.

I should state here that when we say we are fighting for a united, democratic and non-racial South Africa, we mean what we say. It is very clear to us that unless our country becomes such an entity, we shall know no peace. To propose any so-called solutions, which fall within the parameters of the apartheid system is no more than to prepare a recipe for a continuation of the conflict which has already claimed too many lives.

It is to ask for the continued murder and imprisonment of children, which has become a permanent feature of Pretoria's policy of repression. It is to prepare for the extension of the policy of the deliberate impoverishment of the masses of the Black people, the forced removal and banishment of millions, the break-up of families and everything else that you know about the apartheid system.

As long as this system exists, whatever guise it assumes, so long will the Frontline and neighbouring states be victims of aggression and destabilisation. For all this to end, for these crimes to become a thing of the past, South Africa must become a democratic country, with guaranteed liberties for all citizens, with equal rights for everybody regardless of colour, race or sex.

Given the changing balance of strength in our country and the shift of the strategic initiative into our hands, there is a sense in which the apartheid forces are becoming the opposition to the ascendant democratic movement rather than the other way round. The recent White elections demonstrate this point inasmuch as the Botha regime contested them on the specific platform of opposition to the ANC. Subsequent to its victory, this regime has not changed its tune, but has continued with its threats to act vigorously against the democratic movement and has actually carried out these threats as well as murdered a young Zimbabwean woman, who was married to the administrative secretary in our office in Harare.

In the recent period intense debates have arisen about the academic and cultural boycotts. In a critical sense, these debates arise from the successes of our all-round struggle and reflect attempts to get to grips with new dimensions that the emergence of the alternative democratic power entails.

The boycott campaigns, from their inception in the late 'fifties, were aimed at the total isolation of apartheid South Africa. This objective is inviolate and needs to be pursued with even greater vigour.

At the same time, we must take into account the changes that have taken place over time. In particular, as in almost every other field of human endeavour in South Africa, there has emerged a definable, alternative, democratic culture — the People's Culture permeated with and giving expression to the deepest aspirations of our people in struggle, immersed in democratic and enduring human values.

This is a development, however, that is taking place within the context of the emergent alternative democratic power, whose duty it is to draw on the academic and cultural resources and heritage of the world community to advance the democratic perspective in our country. For it is only with the realisation of a non- racial, democratic and united South Africa that such a People's Culture shall be able to flourish in full glory.

To a lesser or greater degree, there has always been a tradition of progressive culture, which has struggled for survival and growth against colonial domination and commercialisation. The change that has occurred is that this People's Culture, despite the extreme hostility of the racist state, has grown into a mighty stream, distinct from and in opposition to the warped and moribund culture of racism. Its foremost exponents are today part of the democratic movement. The core of the cultural workers engaged in creating this People's Culture are simultaneously engaged in developing our own institutions and structures, which are aligned to mass democratic organisations in our country.

As in politics, trade unionism, education, sport, religion and many other fields, these developments at the cultural level both contributed to and are part of the emergent alternative democratic power at whose head stands the ANC.

Without doubt the developing and vibrant culture of our people in struggle and its structures need to be supported, strengthened and enhanced. In the same way as apartheid South Africa is being increasingly isolated internationally, within South Africa this People's Culture is steadily isolating the intellectual and cultural apologists of apartheid.

Indeed, the moment is upon us when we shall have to deal with the alternative structures that our people have created and are creating through struggle and sacrifice as the genuine representatives of these masses in all fields of human activity. Not only should these not be boycotted, but more, they should be supported, encouraged and treated as the democratic counterparts within South Africa of similar institutions and organisations internationally. This means that the ANC, the broad democratic movement in its various formations within South Africa and the international solidarity movement need to act together.

On these questions John Collins entertained no doubts whatsoever. Having taken positions against racism, discrimination, oppression and war, he accepted that to bring these to an end he must march side by side with those of like mind, against the racists, the oppressors and the warmongers. His example is eminently worthy of emulation.

Everywhere in our country, and after a year of national State of Emergency, the democratic forces are at work to expand and strengthen their ranks and to raise the level and intensity of the offensive against the apartheid regime to new heights. For its part, this regime prepares itself for more atrocities, for the campaign of repression of which P.W. Botha boasts — as though to shoot and kill children, to imprison and torture them and their parents to carry out one outrage after another against

124

independent Africa, were the worthiest activities that one could ever imagine.

A terrible collision between ourselves and our opponents is inevitable. Many battles will be fought and many lives will be lost throughout our region. In preparation for this, the Pretoria regime has identified the defeat of the democratic movement as the centrepiece of state policy. Yet the outcome is not in doubt. Having reached the crossroads, the masses of our people have decided that our country must advance as rapidly as possible to the situation where they, Black and White, will govern themselves together as equals. Whatever the cost, there is no doubt that we will win.

We cannot but regret that such titans of our struggle as John Collins will not be with us to celebrate the birth of democracy in our country. In a fortnight you, who are his compatriots, will be casting your votes to choose representatives to your Parliament. How terrible it is that in the Southern tip of Africa, millions have to go through the furnace of violent struggle to win for themselves a right which you take for granted!

What a tragedy that many more will have to die simply because this, a democratic country, refused to heed Canon Collins's plea for his motherland to side with the oppressed and to declare war on the tyrants! What a tragedy that those, who exercise power, have become so bereft of vision that they have learnt to treat as no more than a slogan, the objective of the expansion of the frontiers of democracy to the Black oppressed of Namibia and South Africa!

When freedom comes, what will they say then?

What will they do then?

Will they finally claim Canon Collins as one of their own?

INDIA AND THE STRUGGLE FOR FREEDOM IN SOUTH AFRICA

E.S. REDDY

Text of the paper published by the United Nations Centre against Apartheid in October, 1985.

Introduction

India's contribution to the struggle against apartheid has been highly praised by the leaders of the freedom movement in South Africa. Nelson Mandela, the outstanding leader of that movement, paid a handsome tribute to India and its leaders in a letter smuggled out of Robben Island prison in 1980. Great appreciation has also been expressed by African leaders for the role of India since 1946 in promoting international support for the freedom struggle in South Africa, and its many actions and initiatives in solidarity with the oppressed people of that country.

While such expressions of appreciation are most gratifying, it must be emphasised that the contribution by the Government and the people of India to the freedom movement in South Africa is more than an act of solidarity. It has deep roots in India's own struggle for freedom and dignity.

The humiliations and indignities to which the people of Indian origin were subjected in South Africa, and the struggle for their human dignity led by Mahatma Gandhi, have had a great influence on the Indian national movement. Under the leadership of Mahatma Gandhi and Pandit Jawaharlal Nehru, it developed an international outlook, espousing uncompromising opposition to colonialism and racism and recognising that India's own freedom was meaningless unless all the peoples under colonial and racist domination were free. It felt a particular affinity with the freedom movements in South Africa and other African countries.

Soon after assuming office as Prime Minister in the Interim Government of India, Pandit Nehru declared at a press conference on September 27, 1946:

"The kernel of our policy is the ending of colonialism all over Asia, or for that matter, in Africa and elsewhere and racial equality ... and the end of domination or exploitation of one nation by another."

This he stressed, was the only way to bring about world peace and progress.

While India was concerned with the treatment of people of India origin in South Africa as an affront to the dignity and honour of the nation, he saw the issue in the context of even greater oppression of the African majority. India, therefore, took the lead in ensuring United Nations consideration of apartheid and in promoting solidarity with all the oppressed people.

The Government and people of India have entertained great respect for the liberation movement in South Africa and its leaders, and have been unequivocal in support of their struggle. The contributions made in that cause and in implementation of the United Nations resolutions were never regarded as a sacrifice but as a national duty.

It may be useful to trace the evolution of India's concern and commitment, not only for an understanding of the role of India, but also for pointing to the lessons of its long experience of solidarity with the struggle for liberation in South Africa.

Gandhi in South Africa

"The oldest existing political organisation in South Africa, the Natal Indian Congress, was founded by Mahatma Gandhi in 1894. He became its first Secretary and in 21 years of his stay in South Africa we were to witness the birth of ideas and methods of struggle that have exerted an incalculable influence on the history of the peoples of India and South Africa. Indeed it was on South African soil that Mahatmaji founded and embraced the philosophy of *Satyagarha*."

— Nelson Mandela in a letter from prison in 1980.

After the abolition of slavery, the British settlers in Natal arranged with the Indian Government to recruit indentured labour for their sugar, tea and coffee plantations. Thousands of poor and illiterate Indians[1] were enticed to go to South Africa with promises of attractive wages and repatriation after five years or the right to settle in Natal as free men. The first indentured labourers reached Natal on November 16 1860.[2] They were soon followed by traders and their assistants.

After some time, the Whites faced serious competition from the traders, as well as the labourers, who became successful market gardeners after the expiry of their indenture. They began an agitation to make it impossible for Indians to live in Natal except in semi-slavery as indentured labourers. In 1893, when Natal was granted self-government, the government began to enact a series of discriminatory and restrictive measures against the free Indians.

The Indian traders, who had settled in the Boer Republic of Transvaal were also subjected to similar discrimination, while Indians were excluded from the Orange Free State.

Mohandas Karamchand Gandhi, a young and diffident barrister, arrived in South Africa in 1893 to represent an Indian trader in Natal in a civil suit against an Indian trading firm in Pretoria. Within days, he encountered bitter humiliations such as being pushed out of a train and being assaulted for walking on a footpath. The experience steeled him: he decided never to accept or be resigned to injustice and racism, but to resist.

He helped found the Natal Indian Congress in 1894, bringing together Indians of all classes, speaking a variety of languages, into one organisation to struggle for their rights. It was the first mass organisation in South Africa.[3]

128

Proceeding to India in 1896, he travelled all over the country, publicising the situation in South Africa, meeting leaders of the Indian National Congress, editors and others. When he returned to Durban in January, 1897, he was brutally assaulted by a White mob and barely escaped lynching. The incident was widely reported in India and England and the British government was obliged to instruct the Natal authorities to take action against his assailants. Gandhi refused to prosecute them and went on with his work.

When the Anglo-Boer War broke out in 1899, the British government gave as one of the reasons the discrimination against British subjects of Indian origin in the Transvaal and the Orange Free State. Gandhi organised an ambulance corps on the British side, though he felt sympathy for the Afrikaners. At the end of the war, however, the British administrators enforced more stringent restrictions on the Indians in the Transvaal.

In 1907, the Transvaal government enacted the "Black Act" (Asiatic Registration Act), requiring compulsory registration and finger-printing of Indians. The Indian community defied the law under the leadership of Gandhi, and many were imprisoned in this first *Satyagraha* (non-violent resistance) launched by him. Within a few months, General Smuts agreed to release the prisoners and repeal the Act in return for voluntary registration by the Indians.

But the government broke the promise and maintained the Act, though with some amendments. So the Indian community resumed the struggle in 1908. Thousands of Indians burnt their registration certificates. The *Satyagraha* continued this time for several years, since the Whites, who were negotiating for "self-government", resorted to harassment rather than mass arrests.

Gandhi went in a deputation of Indians to Britain in 1909 to oppose the granting of self-government to the Whites and met many Members of Parliament and public figures. But the British Government ignored the pleas of the Indians — and indeed of the African majority—and transferred power to the White minority in 1910.

Meanwhile, the *Satyagraha* received wide attention in India. Gopal Krishna Gokhale, a prominent national leader, with whom Gandhi was in constant communication, initiated a debate in the Legislative Council of India and secured a resolution to prohibit recruitment of indentured labour for Natal. Subsequently, with British encouragement, Gokhale visited South Africa in 1912 and met General Smuts and General Botha, who undertook to repeal the Black Act and abolish the poll-tax.

But again the undertaking was not kept. Moreover, the Indian community was infuriated at a judgement of the Cape Supreme Court in 1913 declaring all marriages—other than those according to Christian rites and registered with the Registrar of Marriages beyond the pale of law in South Africa.

Gandhi then revived the *Satyagraha* on a much bigger scale, inviting women and indentured labourers to join. Tens of thousands of workers in the Newcastle coal mines and in plantations on the Natal coast went on strike and defied brutal police violence. Thousands of Indians went to gaol.

Public opinion in India reacted strongly and even Lord Hardinge, the Viceroy, criticised the government of the Union of South Africa and expressed his "deep and burning" sympathy for the *Satyagrahis*. There were also protests in Britain.

As a result, General Smuts reached an agreement with Gandhi in January 1914, repealing the poll-tax and validating Indian marriages. This was a compromise, as other discriminatory measures remained, but provided some security for the Indian community. Gandhi suspended the *Satyagraha* and left South Africa in July 1914 as a *Mahatma*.[4]

The experience of Mahatma Gandhi in South Africa had a tremendous influence in India, as he proceeded to develop the Indian National Congress as a mass movement, leading to the independence of the country.

In South Africa, despite his great respect and sympathy for the Africans, his political activities were confined to the Indian community as it was in a particularly vulnerable position. His influence on the freedom movement in that country was, therefore, by example. But as Oliver Tambo said in New Delhi on November 14, 1980: "His imprint on the course of the South African struggle is indelible."

Mahatma Gandhi, moreover, was a great publicist, and the success of *Satyagraha* depended both on the courage and sacrifice of the resisters and on the response of public opinion. He attracted the support of a number of Whites in South Africa, who soon became supporters of the African cause. Public opinion in India was greatly concerned with the Indian National Congress adopting annual resolutions on South Africa. Mahatma Gandhi also helped promote awareness of South African racism in Britain.

Gandhi was in frequent correspondence with people in other countries, including Count Leo Tolstoy, who wrote to him:

"And so your activity in Transvaal, as it seems to us, at the end of the world, is the most essential work now being done in the world, and in which not only the nations of the Christians but of all the world will undoubtedly take part."

The efforts of Mahatma Gandhi thus helped to attract international attention to the issue of racism in South Africa long before the United Nations began considering the matter.

Solidarity of Freedom Movements

"...there is a real moral bond between Asiatics and Africans. It will grow as time passes."

—*Mahatma Gandhi in* **Harijan,** *February 24, 1946*

"It would be a grave omission on our part if we failed to mention the close bonds that have existed between our people and the people of India, and to acknowledge the encouragement, the inspiration and the practical assistance we have received as a result of the international outlook of the All India Congress."

—*Nelson Mandela in his letter from prison*

Under the leadership of Mahatma Gandhi and Pandit Jawaharlal Nehru, the Indian National Congress developed a strong international outlook, with the elimination of colonialism and racism all over the world as the foremost concern, and established contacts with freedom movements in other countries.

Africa had a special place, partly because of the concern of Mahatma Gandhi. Pandit Nehru, for his part, was always passionate in denouncing the humiliation of Africa and felt that Asia had a duty to help Africa regain its dignity and freedom. He said in his address to the Asian Relations Conference in New Delhi on March 23, 1947:

> "We of Asia have a special responsibility to the people of Africa. We must help them to their rightful place in the human family."

And in his concluding statement at the Asian-African Conference in Bandung on April 24, 1955:

> "We have passed resolutions about conditions in this or that country. But I think there is nothing more terrible than the infinite tragedy of Africa in the past few hundred years. Everything else pales into insignificance when I think of the infinite tragedy of Africa ever since the days when millions of Africans were carried away as galley slaves to America and elsewhere, half of them dying in the galleys... Even now the tragedy of Africa is greater than that of any other continent, whether it is racial or political. It is up to Asia to help Africa to the best of her ability because we are sister continents."

There were frequent contacts between Indian and African leaders.[5]

Both Mahatma Gandhi and Pandit Nehru repeatedly stressed the solidarity of Asian and African peoples and advised the Indians in South Africa to identify with the African majority. One of the first acts of Pandit Nehru, after becoming Prime Minister in the Interim Government of India, was to send instructions to Indian envoys in Africa that India did not want Indians to have any special privileges at the cost of Africans anywhere. He called upon the Indians to co-operate with Africans in order to gain freedom for Africans.

132

The bond between the national movements of India and South Africa became stronger during the Second World War.

The Indians in South Africa were no longer recent immigrants, but were born in South Africa and had developed deep roots in that country. With the encouragement of the Indian national movement, they recognised that their destiny was linked to that of the African majority and increasingly participated in joint struggles against racist measures. The militants — from Gandhians to Marxists—under the leadership of Dr Yusuf Dadoo and Dr Monty Naicker, took over leadership of the community from the so-called "moderates" who were compromising with the racist regime, and entered into a pact with Dr A.B. Xuma of the African National Congress of South Africa (ANC). (See Appendix 1 for "Three Doctors' Pact")

Moreover, while the Allies professed to be fighting for freedom, Winston Churchill, the British Prime Minister, made it clear that the Atlantic Charter did not apply to India, while General Smuts, acclaimed in the West as a liberal, was equally determined that equality was not for the Blacks. Freedom had to be wrenched by struggle in both countries.

In India, the national movement launched the final assault against colonial rule in 1942 — the "Quit India" movement under the slogan "Do or Die." In South Africa, the African Youth League was established by young militants calling for "positive action": Nelson Mandela, Oliver Tambo and Walter Sisulu, who are still leading the struggle, were among its founders.

The Indian national movement, which began in the 1880s, and the South African national movement, which began three decades later, developed on parallel lines — in organisation, forms of resistance and ideology — in protracted struggles against powerful forces. India had, therefore, a special appreciation of the concerns and needs of the latter.

Complaint to the UN in 1946

"In South Africa, racialism is the state doctrine and our people are putting up a heroic struggle against the tyranny of a racial minority. If this racial doctrine is going to be tolerated, it must inevitably lead to vast conflicts and world disaster..."

—Pandit Jawaharlal Nehru in a broadcast on September 7, 1946

The complaint by India to the United Nations in 1946 of racial discrimination in South Africa was made before the establishment of a national government, because of strong public sentiment in the country against continuing discrimination against the people of Indian origin.

The Smuts-Gandhi agreement of 1914 gave only a respite to the Indians in South Africa. Anti-Indian agitation was revived by the Whites after the First World War, and the Union Government introduced new discriminatory measures in violation of the agreement. After protests from India, talks were held between the colonial Government of India and the Union Government: a compromise was reached in the Cape Town Agreement of 1927 and confirmed by a joint communique of 1932. These agreements were also virtually repudiated by South Africa.

In 1943, Natal passed the "Pegging Act", restricting the right of Asians to acquire land. Then, in 1946, the Union Government passed the Asiatic Land Tenure and Indian Representation Act to segregate Indians in trade and residence. The Indian community launched a passive resistance campaign on June 13, 1946. Many Indian men and women were imprisoned by the police or assaulted by White gangsters.

In response to public pressure in India, the Government of India felt obliged to request the United Nations General Assembly, in a letter of June 22, 1946, to consider the question of the treatment of Indians in the Union of South Africa. At that time, South Africa accounted for 5.5 per cent of India's exports, and about 1.5 per cent of India's imports.

The Interim Government was established on September 1, 1946, before the General Assembly session, with Pandit Jawaharlal Nehru as Prime Minister. The new government made sure to emphasise the wider context of the dispute between India and the Union of South Africa. It resisted moves by the Western Powers to deal with the Indian complaint as a legal problem and insisted on its consideration as a political matter.

(Mrs) Vijayalakshmi Pandit, Chairman of the Indian delegation in 1946, said in her opening statement:

"...The way this Assembly treats and disposes of this issue is open to the gaze, not only of those gathered here, but of millions of people in the world, the progressive peoples of all countries, more particularly the non-European peoples of the world — who...are an overwhelming section of the human race.

"This issue we have brought before you is by no means a narrow or local one...

"The bitter memories of racial doctrines in the practice of states and governments are still fresh in the minds of all of us. Their evil and tragic consequences are part of the problems with which we are called upon to deal.

"India firmly believes that imperialism, political, economic or social, in whatever part of the world it may exist and by whomsoever it may be established and perpetuated, is totally inconsistent with the objects and purposes of the United Nations and its Charter."

During the session, a multiracial delegation from South Africa led by Dr A.B. Xuma, President-General of the ANC, and including H.A. Naidoo of the Natal Indian Congress and H.M. Bassner, Senator representing African voters, arrived in New York. The Indian delegation constantly consulted them and enabled them to contact many governments. V.K. Krishna Menon, a member of the delegation, shared the platform with them on November 17, 1946 at a public meeting in the Abyssinian Baptist Church in Harlem.

Because of the composition of the United Nations, it was with great difficulty that India was able to secure a two-thirds majority for a resolution on its complaint.

At the same session, India played an active role in opposing and frustrating the manoeuvres of the South African government to annex South West Africa (now Namibia). It strongly supported a resolution moved by Poland and Egypt against religious and so-called racial discrimination.

India became the target of vicious propaganda by the South African government and earned the disfavour of its Western friends.

The annual discussions of the Indian complaint built up a sentiment against racial discrimination in South Africa, and against apartheid, which became official policy after the National Party came to power in 1948.

Initiative on Apartheid

On June 26, 1952, the ANC, the South African Indian Congress and the Coloured People's Organisation launched a non-violent "Campaign of Defiance against Unjust Laws" in which 8,000 people of all races were imprisoned for contravention of discriminatory laws.

At the request of the freedom movement, India, together with 12 other Asian and Arab States, called on the General Assembly to consider the wider issue under the title "Question of race conflict in South Africa resulting from the policies of apartheid of the government of the Union of South Africa." Their explanatory memorandum deserves to be recalled. They said:

> "The race conflict in the Union of South Africa resulting from the policies of apartheid of the South African government is creating a dangerous and explosive situation, which constitutes both a threat to international peace and a flagrant violation of the basic principles of human rights and fundamental freedoms which are enshrined in the Charter of the United Nations.

> "Although Africa's importance in world affairs is increasing rapidly, many parts of that continent still remain subject to racial discrimination and exploitation. The founding of the United Nations and the acceptance by the Member States of the obligations embodied in the Charter have given to peoples of these areas new hope and encouragement in their efforts to acquire basic human rights. But, in direct opposi-

136

tion to the trend of world opinion, the policy of the government of the Union of South Africa is designed to establish and to perpetuate every form of racial discrimination, which must inevitably result in intense and bitter racial conflict...

"...a social system is being evolved under which the non-Whites, who constitute 80 per cent of the population of the Union of South Africa, will be kept in a permanently inferior state to the White minority. Such a policy challenges all that the United Nations stands for and clearly violates the basic and fundamental objectives of the Charter of the United Nations...

"It is, therefore, imperative that the General Assembly give this question its urgent consideration in order to prevent an already dangerous situation from deteriorating further and to bring about a settlement in accordance with the purposes and principles of the United Nations Charter."

To stress the importance attached by India to this issue, leaders of the Indian delegation personally led the annual debates until 1957 (when, with the independence of Ghana, India requested Ghana to take the lead). For, India recognised apartheid as a unique and grave menace to peace, rather than one of the many human rights violations in the world.

Pandit Nehru said in the Lok Sabha in April, 1958:

"There are many conflicts which divide the world and this question of racial conflict in South Africa is as grave as any other issue.

"In South Africa, it is the deliberate, acknowledged and loudly proclaimed policy of the government itself to maintain this segregation and racial discrimination. This makes the South African case unique in the world. It is a policy with which obviously no person and no country, which believes in the United Nations Charter can ever compromise, because it uproots almost everything the modern world stands for and considers worthwhile, whether it is the United Nations Charter or whether it is our ideas of democracy or of human dignity."

While the original Indian complaint remained on the agenda of the General Assemply for several years, Pandit Nehru recognised that it had become part of the larger issue. He said in a speech in the Rajya Sabha on December 15, 1958:

"The question of the people of Indian descent in South Africa has really merged into bigger questions, where not only Indians are affected but the whole African population along with ... any other people who happen to go to South Africa and who do not belong to European or American countries."

He said in the Lok Sabha on March 28, 1960, after the Sharpeville massacre:

"The people of Indian descent in South Africa, as we all know, have had to put up with a great deal of discrimination and suffering and we have resented that. But we must remember that the African people have to put up with something infinitely more and that, therefore, our sympathies must go out to them even more than to our kith and kin there."

The two items were merged in 1962 under the title "Policies of Apartheid of the Government of the Republic of South Africa."

India joined the African states in calling for Security Council discussion of apartheid after the Sharpeville massacre of 1960. It co-sponsored the General Assembly resolution of 1962 urging all states to impose sanctions against South Africa and establishing the Special Committee against Apartheid.

In the specialised agencies of the United Nations, in the Movement of Non-Aligned countries and the Commonwealth, as well as in numerous other organisations and forums, India was active in calling for the isolation of the apartheid regime and support for the liberation struggle.

Support to Africa

"The decade of the 'eighties may well decide the destiny of Southern Africa. The African people must win. And we, in India, reiterate our total support to you."

— Prime Minister Indira Gandhi, in an address to the African Students Association in New Delhi, January 11, 1982.

"This is the time when all the non-White people of South Africa, and even those sections among the Whites who oppose apartheid should close their ranks and fight unitedly to vanquish the racist policies. The people of India will be with them."

— Prime Minister Rajiv Gandhi, in a statement on August 16, 1985.

By the early 1960s, the independent African States were able to take over the responsibility for promoting support to peoples fighting against colonial and racist domination, recognising that their cause was that of the entire continent.

India lent full support to African States and the Organisation of African Unity (OAU). It set an example by scrupulously implementing the resolutions of the United Nations and other international organisations. It also provided substantial assistance to the oppressed people of South Africa and their freedom movement. Thus, while India gladly handed over leadership to African states, its role was hardly passive.

In recent years, India has been obliged to assume a more active role, with the encouragement of African states, because of its chairmanship of the Non-Aligned Movement and the difficulties encountered by African states.

Indira Gandhi had seen the humiliation of Africans and Asians in South Africa as she was obliged to stop in South Africa in 1930-1931 on her way home from England. She was passionate in her hatred of apartheid and entertained great respect for the leaders of the resistance. She told the African Students Association in New Delhi on January 11, 1982:

"... we regard Nelson Mandela as one of the foremost proponents of freedom — freedom of man. We regard him also as a friend of India. We admire him. We have honoured him as one of our own heroes and our thoughts are often with him and his family...."

As the Prime Minister of India and as the Chairperson of the

Non-Aligned Movement, she devoted special attention to the freedom of Southern Africa. Her appeal to the people of South Africa in 1984 not to cooperate with the racist constitution designed to divide the Black people was of great significance in frustrating the manoeuvres of the Botha regime and promoting united mass resistance in South Africa.

Rajiv Gandhi, her son and successor, has shown an equally strong commitment to the cause of freedom in South Africa — both in his statements and in actions taken by his Government.

Some Observations

India has been privileged to play a special role in support of the long and difficult struggle of the Black majority in South Africa for freedom and human dignity. Solidarity with the South African movement is an issue on which all segments of public opinion in India are united.

Having gone through a long struggle for independence, India has always entertained faith in the triumph of the liberation struggle in South Africa. It also showed full understanding, in the light of her own experience, when the freedom movement in South Africa was obliged to abandon strict adherence to non-violence.

India's long experience with South Africa has influenced its approach to apartheid.

For India, the distinction between colonial and racial problems in Southern Africa has little basis. In South Africa, racism became the "State" policy because the colonial power, ignoring the pleas of the African majority and the Indian population, handed over power to a White minority intent on reinforcing racist domination and exploitation.

India is also not influenced by propaganda describing Afrikaners as racists and English-speaking Whites as liberals. For, the Indians in South Africa suffered discrimination from the English-speaking Whites in Natal as much as from the Afrikaners in the Transvaal.

Aware of the long record of breaches of undertaking by the racist authorities, India fully appreciates that the Black people can have little faith in the so-called "reforms" by the apartheid regime. It rejects appeasement of the racist regime and recognises that the transition to a non-racial society will need to be under the leadership of the genuine leaders of the people.

As Prime Minister Rajiv Gandhi said on August 19, 1985:

"South Africa must be made to see reason. It must be made to release Nelson Mandela unconditionally. The only way this can be done is to isolate totally the racists. It is futile to hope that cooperation in any manner with that regime will give anyone leverage or influence, so as to change things for the better."

While the experience of India is, perhaps, unique, it has relevance for other states that have been seized with the problem of apartheid at least since the United Nations bagan to discuss it in 1952.

South Africa is a microcosm of the world with people of different national and racial origins. The racist regime in that country has been pursuing a criminal, indeed suicidal policy, while the freedom movement has consistently espoused the need to establish a just and non-racial society.

India, with a million people in South Africa tracing their origin to it, has made a clear choice in total support of the liberation struggle. Why is it that other countries of origin—especially of the White minority — are unwilling to make such a choice and act accordingly? Why is it that some of them even use their historic links as a justification for collusion with apartheid to the detriment of all the people of South Africa?

India, a poor country, gave up over five per cent of its export trade in 1946 to demonstrate its repugnance of racism in South Africa. Why is it that the major trading partners of South Africa are unwilling to give up even one per cent or less of their trade? Are they less committed to the struggle against racism?

The leaders of India have educated public opinion on the situation in South Africa and secured full support for all measures recommended by the United Nations. Why it is that governments in the West are still resisting demands of public opinion in their own countries for action against apartheid.

India, a country, which suffered from alien domination and exploitation, has accepted responsibility to assist Africa in its striving for total emancipation from centuries of humiliation. Why is it that governments of countries that ravaged and plundered Africa seem unwilling to shoulder their moral responsibility?

It is to be hoped that the heroic struggle now being waged by the men, women and children of all racial origins in South Africa will persuade the governments concerned to re-assess their positions and contribute fully to the international efforts for the eradication of apartheid.

NOTES

1. The term "Indians" is used in South Africa to denote people from the Indian sub-continent. Most of them trace their origin to the states of Tamil Nadu, Andhra Pradesh and Gujarat in the Republic of India.

2. Some Indians had arrived in South Africa long before the indentured labourers, having been brought as slaves, and became part of the "Coloured" community. Dr Abdurrahman, a prominent "Coloured" leader early this century, was a descendant of a slave from Bengal.

3. Several of its leaders are now under trial for treason for their non-violent resistance to apartheid in association with the United Democratic Front (UDF).

4. Before leaving South Africa, Gandhi sent as a gift to General Smuts a pair of sandals he made in jail. Recalling this in 1939, General Smuts wrote: "I have worn these sandals for many a summer since then, even though I may feel that I am not worthy to stand in the shoes of so great a man."

5. For instance, Mahatma Gandhi attended the All Races Conference held in London in 1911, together with African leaders of South Africa. Pandit Nehru represented the Indian

National Congress at the International Congress against Imperialism held in Brussels in 1927. This conference was also attended by the President of the ANC of South Africa J.T. Gumede. The India League in London maintained close contact with African exiles in London and several Indians attended the Pan African Congress held in Manchester in 1945.

APPENDIX 1

Three Doctors' Pact

The following is the text of the "Joint Declaration of Cooperation" signed by Dr. A.B. Xuma of the African National Congress, Dr. G.M. Naicker of the Natal Indian Congress and Dr. Y.M. Dadoo of the Transvaal Indian Congress, 40 years ago on March 9, 1947.

"This Joint Meeting between the representatives of the African National Congress and the Natal and Transvaal Indian Congresses, having fully realised the urgency of cooperation between the Non-European peoples and other democratic forces for the attainment of basic human rights and full citizenship for all sections of the South African people, has resolved that a Joint Declaration of Cooperation is imperative for the working out of a practical basis of cooperation between the National Organisations of the Non-European peoples.

"This Joint Meeting declares its sincerest conviction that for the future progress, goodwill, good race relations, and for the building of a united greater and free South Africa, full franchise rights must be extended to all sections of the South African people, and to this end, this Joint Meeting pledges the fullest cooperation between the African and Indian peoples and appeals to all democratic and freedom-loving citizens of South Africa to support fully and cooperate in this struggle for:

1. Full Franchise.

2. Equal economic and industrial rights and opportunities and the recognition of African Trade Unions under the Industrial Conciliation Act.

3. The removal of all land restrictions against Non-Europeans and the provision of adequate housing facilities for all Non-Europeans.

4. The extension of free and compulsory education to Non-Europeans.

5. Guaranteeing freedom of movement and the abolition of Pass Laws against the African people and the provincial barriers against Indians.

6. And the removal of all discriminatory and oppressive legislations from the Union's Statute Book.

"This Joint Meeting is, therefore, of the opinion that for the attainment of these objects it is urgently necessary that a vigorous campaign be immediately launched and that every effort be made to compel the Union Government to implement the United Nations' decisions and to treat the Non-European peoples in South Africa in conformity with the principles of the United Nations Charter.

"This Joint Meeting further resolves to meet from time to time to implement this Declaration and to take active steps in proceeding with the campaign."

The Freedom Charter

On June 25 and 26, 1955, at Kliptown, a small town near Johannesburg, the "Freedom Charter" was unanimously adopted by over 3,000 delegates of all ethnic groups — Africans, Coloureds, Indians and Whites. The Charter, since then, has come to be accepted as a document which expresses the basic aims and aspirations of the ANC, the mass democratic movement and the people of South Africa. In recent years, the Charter, inspite of being a banned document, has been increasingly adopted by various religious, social, cultural and political organisations as a document reflecting their own vision of a future South Africa.

For nearly 18 months prior to the "Congress of the People," thousands of meetings were held all over the country, where the peoples' demands were discussed for inclusion in the Freedom Charter and delegates elected. At the historic Congress, the Freedom Charter was read out clause by clause, discussed and finally adopted unanimously. Besides English, it was translated into the major languages of the country — Zulu, Xhosa, Sotho, Afrikans, etc.

As the Congress was about to disperse in the evening of June 26, hundreds of police with sten-guns marched in and surrounded the open-air gathering. Every delegate's and participant's name and address was taken on the pretext that treason was being investigated. A year-and-a-half later, on December 5, 1956, 156 South Africans of all nationalities were arrested in a country-wide swoop at dawn on allegations of "high treason." In the prolonged trial lasting for nearly five years, the Freedom Charter and the Congress of the People featured prominently in the State's case. Though all the accused were found not guilty and discharged many were to be subsequently harrassed, persecuted, banned, banished or house-arrested and some, like Nelson Mandela, Walter Sisulu, Ahmed Kathrada and Lionel Bernstein were to be charged for sabotage in the 1963/64 Rivonia Trial. Mandela, Sisulu, Kathrada, Mbeki and others were sentenced to life imprisonment for plotting the "violent overthrow of the State."

We, the People of South Africa, declare for all our country and the world to all our country and the world to know:

That South Africa belongs to all who live in it, Black and White, and that no government can justly claim authority, unless it is based on the will of all the people;

That our people have been robbed of their birthright to land, liberty and peace by a form of government founded on injustice and inequality;

That our country will never be prosperous or free until all our people live in brotherhood, enjoying equal rights and opportunities;

That only a democratic state, based on the will or all the people, can secure to all their birthright without distinction of colour, race, sex or belief;

And therefore, we, the people of South Africa, Black and White together — equals, countrymen and brothers — adopt this Freedom Charter. And we pledge ourselves to strive together, sparing neither strength nor courage, until the democratic changes here set out have been won.

The People Shall Govern!

Every man and woman shall have the right to vote for and to stand as a candidate for all bodies which make laws;

All people shall be entitled to take part in the administration of the country.

147

The rights of the people shall be the same, regardless of race, colour or sex;

All bodies of minority rule, advisory boards, councils and authorities shall be replaced by democratic organs of self-government.

All National Groups Shall have Equal Rights!

There shall be equal status in the bodies of state, in the courts and in the schools for all national groups and races;

All people shall have equal right to use their own languages, and to develop their own folk culture and customs;

All national groups shall be protected by law against insults to their race and national pride;

The preaching and practice of national, race or colour discrimination and contempt shall be a punishable crime;

All apartheid laws and practices shall be set aside;

All shall be free to travel without restriction from countryside to town, from province to province, and from South Africa abroad;

Pass Laws, permits and all other laws restricting these freedoms shall be abolished.

Their Shall be Work and Security!

All who work shall be free to form trade unions, to elect their officers and to make wage agreements with their employers;

The state shall recognise the right and duty of all to work and to draw full unemployment benefits;

Men and women of all races shall receive equal pay for equal work;

There shall be a forty-hour working week, a national minimum wage, paid annual leave and sick leave for all workers, and maternity leave on full pay for all working mothers;

Miners, domestic workers, farm workers and civil servants shall have the same rights as all others who work.

Child labour, compound labour, the lot system and contract labour shall be abolished.

The Doors of Learning and of Culture shall be Opened!

The government shall discover, develop and encourage national talent for the enhancement of our cultural life;

All the cultural treasures of mankind shall be open to all, by free exchange of books, ideas and contact with other lands;

The aim of education shall be to teach the youth to ove their people and their culture, to honour human brotherhood, liberty and peace;

Education shall be free, compulsory, universal and equal for all children;

Higher education and technical training shall be opened to all by means of state allowances and scholarships awarded on the basis of merit;

Adult illiteracy shall be ended by a mass state education plan.

The People shall Share in the Country's Wealth!

The national wealth of our country, the heritage of all South Africans, shall be restored to the people;

The mineral wealth beneath the soil, the banks and monopoly industry shall be transferred to the ownership of the people as a whole;

All other industry and trade shall be controlled to assist the well-being of the people;

All people shall have equal rights to trade where they choose, to manufacture and to enter all trades, crafts and professions.

The Land shall be Shared Among those who Work it!

Restrictions of land ownership on a racial basis shall be ended, and all the land re-divided amongst those who work it, to banish famine and land hunger;

The state shall help the peasants with implements, seed, tractors and dams to save the soil and assist the tillers;

Freedom of movement shall be guaranteed to all who work on the land;

All shall have the right to occupy land wherever they choose;

People shall not be robbed of their cattle and forced labour and farm prisons shall be abolished.

All shall be Equal Before the Law!

No one shall be imprisoned, deported or restricted without a fair trial;

No one shall be condemned by the order of any government official;

The courts shall be representative of all the people;

Imprisonment shall be only for serious crimes against the people, and shall aim at re-education, not vengeance;

The police force and army shall be open to all, on an equal basis and shall be the helpers and protectors of the people;

All laws, which discriminate on grounds of race, colour or belief, shall be repealed.

All shall Enjoy Equal Human Rights!

The law shall guarantee to all their right to speak, to organise, to meet together, to publish, to preach, to worship and to educate their children;

The privacy of the house from police raids shall be protected by law;

All shall be free to travel without restriction from countryside to town, from province to province, and from South Africa abroad;

Pass Laws, permits and all other laws restricting these freedoms shall be abolished.

There Shall be Work and Security!

All who work shall be free to form trade unions, to elect their officers and to make wage agreements with their employers;

150

The state shall recognise the right and duty of all to work, and to draw full unemployment benefits;

Men and women of all races shall receive equal pay for equal work;

There shall be a forty-hour working week, a national minimum wage, paid annual leave, and sick leave for all workers, and maternity leave on full pay for all working mothers;

Miners, domestic workers, farm workers and civil servants shall have the same rights as all others who work;

Child labour, compound labour, the tot system and contract labour shall be abolished.

The Doors of Learning and of Culture shall be Opened!

The government shall discover, develop and encourage national talent for the enhancement of our cultural life;

All the cultural treasures of mankind shall be open to all, by free exchange of books, ideas and contact with other lands;

The aim of education shall be to teach the youth to love their people and their culture, to honour human brotherhood, liberty and peace;

Education shall be free, compulsory, universal and equal for all children;

Higher education and technical training shall be opened to all by means of state allowances and scholarships awarded on the basis of merit;

Adult illiteracy shall be ended by a mass state education plan;

Teachers shall have all the rights of other citizens;

The colour bar in cultural life, in sport and in education shall be abolished.

There shall be Houses, Security and Comfort!

All people shall have the right to live where they choose, to be decently housed, and to bring up their families in comfort and security;

Unused housing space to be made available to the people;

Rent and prices shall be lowered, food plentiful and no one shall go hungry;

A preventive health scheme shall be run by the state;

Free medical care and hospitalisation shall be provided for all, with special care for mothers and young children;

Slums shall be demolished and new suburbs built where all have transport, roads, lighting, playing fields, creches and social centres;

The aged, the orphans, the disabled and the sick shall be cared for by the state;

Rest, leisure and recreation shall be the right of all;

Fenced locations and ghettoes shall be abolished, and laws which break up families shall be repealed.

There shall be Peace and Friendship!

South Africa shall be a fully independent state, which respects the rights and sovereignty of all nations;

South Africa shall strive to maintain world peace and the settlement of all international disputes by negotiation — not war;

Peace and friendship amongst all our people shall be secured by upholding the equal rights, opportunities and status of all;

The people of the protectorates — Basutoland, Bechuanaland and Swaziland shall be free to decide for themselves their own future;

The right of all the peoples of Africa to independence and self-government shall be recognised, and shall be the basis of close cooperation.

Let all who love their people and their country now say, as we say here: "THESE FREEDOMS WE WILL FIGHT FOR, SIDE BY SIDE, THROUGHOUT OUR LIVES, UNTIL WE HAVE WON OUR LIBERTY."

Nelson Mandela's Appeal to the People

Message from Nelson Mandela sumggled out of Robben Island and released by the ANC on June 13, 1980

Introduction by Oliver Tambo

The African National Congress of South Africa brings you this urgent call to unity and mass action by political prisoners on Robben Island, to all patriots of our Motherland. Nelson Mandela and hundreds of our comrades have been in the racist regime's prisons for more than 17 years. This message by Nelson Mandela addressed to the struggling masses was written to deal with the present crisis gripping our enemy and in the aftermath of the Soweto uprisings. It was smuggled out of Robben Island under very difficult conditions and has taken over two years to reach us. Nonetheless, we believe the message remains fresh and valid and should be presented to our people. His call to unity and mass action is of particular importance in this Year of the Charter, the 25th anniversary of the Freedom Charter. The ANC urges you to respond to this call and make 1980 a year of united mass struggle.

Mandela's Message

The gun has played an important part in our history. The resistance of the Black man to White colonial intrusion was crushed by the gun. Our struggle to liberate ourselves from White domination is held in check by force of arms. From conquest to the present, the story is the same. Successive White regimes have repeatedly massacred unarmed defenceless Blacks. And, wherever and whenever they have pulled out their guns, the ferocity of their fire has been trained on the African people. Apartheid is the embodiment of the racialism, repression and inhumanity of all previous White supremacist regimes. To see the real face of apartheid, we must look beneath the veil of constitutional formulas, deceptive phrases and playing with words. The rattle of gunfire and the rumbling of Hippo armoured vehicles since June 1976, have once again torn aside the veil. Spread across the face of out country, in Black townships, the racist army and police have been pouring a hail of bullets, killing and maiming hundreds of Black men, women and children.

The toll of the dead and injured already surpasses that of all past massacres carried out by this regime. Apartheid is the rule of the gun and the hangman. The Hippo, the rifle and the gallows are its true symbols. These remain the easiest resort, the ever-ready solution of the race-men rulers of South Africa.

In the midst of the present crisis, while our people count the dead and nurse the injured, they ask themselves: What lies ahead? From our rulers, we can expect nothing. They are the ones who give orders to the soldier crouching over his rifle, theirs is the spirit that moves the finger that caresses the trigger. Vague promises, tinkerings with the machinery of apartheid, constitution juggling, massive arrests and detentions, side by side with renewed overtures aimed a weakening and forestalling the unity of us Blacks and dividing the forces of change — these are the fixed paths along which they will move. For, they are neither capable nor willing to heed the verdict of the masses of our people.

The verdict is loud and clear: Apartheid has failed. Our people remain unequivocal in its rejection. The young and the old, parent and child, all reject it. At the forefront of the 1976/1977 wave of unrest were our students and youth. They come from the universities, high schools and even primary schools. They are a generation, whose whole education has been under the diabolical design of the racists to poison the minds and brain-wash our children into docile subjects of apartheid rule. But after more than 20 years of Bantu Education, the circle is closed and nothing demonstrates the utter bankruptcy of apartheid as the revolt of our youth. The evils, the cruelty and the inhuman-ity of apartheid have been there from its inception. And Blacks, Africans, Coloured and Indians, have opposed it all along the line. What is now unmistakable, what the current wave of unrest has sharply highlighted is this: That, despite all the window-dressing and smooth talk, apartheid has become intol-erable. This awareness reaches over and beyond the particulars of our enslavement. The measure of this truth is the recogni-tion by our people that under apartheid, our lives, individually and collectively, count for nothing.

We face an enemy that is deep-rooted, an enemy entrenched and determined not to yield. Our march to freedom is long and difficult. But both within and beyond our borders the prospects of victory grow bright. The first condition for victory is Black unity. Every effort to divide the Blacks, to woo and pit one Black group against another, must be vigorously repulsed. Our people — African, Indian, Coloured and democratic Whites — must be united into a single massive and solid wall of resistance, of united mass action. Our struggle is growing sharper. This is not the time for the luxury of division and disunity. At all levels and in every walk of life, we must close ranks. Within the ranks of the people, differences must be submerged to the achievement of a single goal — the complete overthrow of apartheid and race domination.

The revulsion of the world against apartheid is growing and the frontiers of White supremacy are shrinking. Mozambique and Angola are free and the war of liberation gathers force in Namibia and Zimbabwe. The soil of our country is destined to be the scene of the fiercest fight and the sharpest battles to rid our continent of the last vestiges of White minority rule. The world is on our side. The OAU, the United Nations and the Anti-Apartheid movement continue to put pressure on the racist rulers of our country. Every effort to isolate South Africa adds strength to our struggle. At all levels of our struggle, within and outside the country, much has been achieved and much remains to be done. But victory is cretain!

We who are confined within the grey walls of the Pretoria regime's prisons reach out to our people. With you, we count those who have perished by means of the gun and the hangman's rope. We salute all of you — the living, the injured and the dead, for you have dared to rise up the tyrant's might. Even as we bow at their graves, we remember this: The dead live on as martyrs in our hearts and minds, a reproach to our disunity and the host of shortcomings that accompany the oppressed, a spur to our efforts to close ranks and a reminder that the freedom of our people is yet to be won. We face the future with confidence. For the guns that serve apartheid cannot render it unconquerable. Those who live by the gun shall perish by the gun.

Between the anvil of united action and the hammer of the armed struggle we shall crush apartheid and White minority racist rule.

Amandla Ngawethu! Matla ke a Rona!

Manifesto of "Umkhonto we Sizwe" (Spear of the Nation) The People's Army

Issued on December 16, 1961

Units of Umkhonto we Sizwe today carried out planned attacks against government installations, particularly those connected with the policy of apartheid and race discrimination.

Umkhonto we Sizwe is a new independent body, formed by Africans. It includes in its ranks South Africans of all races. It is not connected in any way with a so-called "Committee for National Liberation", whose existence has been announced in the press.

Umkhonto we Sizwe will carry on the struggle for freedom and democracy by new methods, which are necessary to complement the actions of the established national liberation movement, and our members, jointly and individually, place themselves under the overall political guidance of that movement.

It is however well known that the main national liberation organisations in this country have consistently followed a policy of non-violence. They have conducted themselves peaceably at all times, regardless of government attacks and persecutions upon them, and despite all government-inspired attempts to provoke them to violence. They have done so because the people prefer peaceful methods of change to achieve their aspirations without the suffering and bitterness of civil war. But the people's patience is not endless.

The time comes in the life of any nation when there remains only two choices: submit or fight. That time has now come to South Africa. We shall not submit and we have no choice but to hit back by all means within our power in defence of our people, our future and our freedom.

The government has interpreted the peacefulness of the movement as weakness; the peoples' non-violent policies have been taken as a green light for government violence. Refusal to resort to force has been interpreted by the government as an invitation to use armed force against the people without reprisals. The methods of Umkhonto we Sizwe mark a break with the past.

We are striking out along a new road for the liberation of the people of this country. The government policy of force, repression and violence will no longer be met with non-violent resistance only! The choice is not ours; it has been made by the Nationalist Government, which has rejected every peaceable demand by the people for rights and freedom and answered every such demand with force and yet more force! Twice in the past 18 months, virtual martial law has been imposed in order to beat down peaceful, non-violent strike action of the people in support of their rights. It is now preparing its forces—enlarging and re-arming its armed forces and drawing the White civilian population into commandos and pistol clubs — for full-scale military actions against the people. The Nationalist Government has chosen the course of force and massacre, now, deliberately, as it did in Sharpeville.

Umkhonto we Sizwe will be at the frontline of the people's defence. It will be the fighting arm of the people against the government and its policies of race oppression. It will be the striking force of the people for liberty, for rights and for their final liberation! Let the government, its supporters who put it into power, and those whose passive toleration of reaction keeps it in power, take note of where the Nationalist Government is leading the country!

We of Umkhonto we Sizwe have always sought—as the liberation movement has sought to achieve liberation, without bloodshed and civil clash. We do still. We hope -- even at this late hour

— that our first actions will awaken everyone to realisation of the disastrous situation to which the Nationalist Government policy is leading. We hope that we will bring the government and its supporters to their senses, before it is too late, so that both the government and its policies can be changed before matters reach the desperate stage of civil war. We believe our actions to be a blow against the Nationalist preparations for civil war and military rule.

In these actions, we are working in the best interests of all the peoples of this country — Black, Brown and White — whose future happiness and well-being cannot be attained without the overthrow of the Nationalist Government, the abolition of White supremacy and the winning of liberty, democracy and full national rights and equality for all the people of this country.

We appeal for the support and encouragement of all those South Africans, who seek the happiness and freedom of the people in this country.

Afrika Mayibuye! (Come Back, Africa!)

(Issued by the command of Umkhonto we Sizwe.)

APPENDIX 5

Oliver Tambo's Appeal

On the occasion of the 75th Anniversary of the African National Congress

On the January 8, 1987, we observed the 75th Anniversary of our movement, the African National Congress. This historic anniversary has come at a critical moment in the struggle for the liberation of our country. Its observance will give both our membership and the people of our country as a whole an opportunity to adopt new initiatives aimed at making further advances toward the birth of a democratic South Africa.

The continuing struggle inside our country combined with the inspiring actions taken by the international community against racist South Africa, have driven the apartheid system into a deep and worsening crisis. Inside our country, the balance of strength between the forces of democracy on the one hand and those of racism on the other has shifted to such an extent that our victory over the apartheid regime is now in sight.

That confidence in the certainty of victory continues to inspire our people to carry out great feats of heroism in the struggle to liberate South Africa and bring peace to our region. The heightened offensive for democracy that has gripped our country for more than two years now is both onstoppable and irreversible.

In the face of these developments, the apartheid regime finds itself with no alternative but to admit the utter bankruptcy of its policy and resort to extreme measures of repression that are doomed to failure. All its actions are those of a regime that is fighting for its very survival.

Indeed, the 75 years of our existence have been characterised by resistance and survival against heavy odds. We have survived martial law and states of emergency. We have been hounded, abducted, raided and massacred in various countries only to emerge, each time, stronger and more resolute to rid our country and the world of the scourge of apartheid.

It is, therefore, most appropriate that as we observe the 75th Anniversary of our movement throughout the year, we should focus our attention on the central question of the destruction of the oppressive and evil system of White minority colonial domination and its replacement by a new democratic and non-racial political and social order.

To do this, and inspired by the greatly increased strength of the democratic movement in South Africa and the anti-apartheid movement internationally as compared to the increasing weakness of the apartheid regime, we must mount the most massive all-round offensive that the apartheid system has ever faced. Our own people are ready to confront this challenge.

We appeal to the world community to join us in this effort. Let the nations across the face of the globe impose comprehensive sanctions against apartheid South Africa. Let the people of the world not only isolate the racists, but also reject their criminal regime as illegitimate.

Let us see the entire peace-loving humanity rally behind the ANC and the rest of the democratic movement of our country. Let us see not only greatly increased moral and material support to the forces of liberty and peace in South Africa but also their recognition as the genuine representatives of the people of our country.

Let the peoples of the world further increase their support for SWAPO and the people of Namibia in their struggle to liberate their country from apartheid colonialism and military occupation. Let all rally to the support of the Frontline States and other states of Southern Africa to help them withstand Pretoria's campaign of aggression and destabilisation.

We are certain that if together we take these measures, we will make a decisive movement forward towards the birth of a free South Africa, an independent Namibia and a peaceful, secure and stable region of Southern Africa. The masses of our people have no doubt whatsoever at this time of great hope and confidence in the future that the international community will march side by side with us to transform the retreat of the enemy into a rout.

Forward to the 75th Anniversary of the African National Congress!

Democracy will triumph!

Victory is certain!

Measures taken by India for the Elimination of Apartheid

PLEA FOR INTERNATIONAL ACTION

Almost 40 years ago, India took the initiative to secure United Nations consideration of the problem of racism in South Africa.

On June 22, 1948, the Government of India requested the General Assembly to consider the question of the treatment of Indians in the Union of South Africa, in the light of discriminatory measures enforced against them in contravention of agreements between the two Governments and the purposes and principles of the Charter of the United Nations. The matter was first considered by the General Assembly during the second part of its first session which began in September, 1946. Although the reference was to the treatment of people of Indian origin, India made it clear its concern over the whole problem of racial discrimination in South Africa. The annual discussions helped build up world public opinion over the broader issue.

On June 26, 1952, the African National Congress of South Africa (ANC), the South African Indian Congress and the Coloured People's Organisation launched the Campaign of Defiance Against Unjust Laws, a non-violent resistance movement in which over 8,000 people of all races were imprisoned for defying racist laws.

India, along with 12 other Asian and Arab States, requested the General Assembly to consider the "question of race conflict in South Africa resulting from the policies of apartheid of the Government of the Union of South Africa." The delegation of India led the discussion on this item until 1957.

In cooperation with African States, India pressed the specialised agencies of the United Nations to take action against apartheid.

Moreover, India has actively supported the struggle against apartheid in other organisations of which it is a member, such as the Commonwealth and the Non-Aligned Movement. It lent strong support to the cause of the South African people at the Asian-African Conference of Bandung in April, 1955, and played an important role in ensuring the exclusion of South Africa from the Commonwealth in 1961.

SANCTIONS AGAINST SOUTH AFRICA

In July 1946, India prohibited trade with South Africa by a Gazette notification No. 2-C(6)/(I and II) dated July 17, 1946, issued by its Department of Commerce. It prohibited the carriage by sea or by land into India of all goods that had been consigned from or grown, produced or manufactured in the Union of South Africa with certain minor exceptions such as personal effects of passengers, newspapers, magazines, etc. Similarly, it prohibited the taking out of India either by sea or by land of goods that were destined for any port or place in the Union of South Africa or in respect of which the Chief Customs Officer was satisfied that the goods, although destined for a port of place outside the Union of South Africa, were intended to be taken to the Union of South Africa.

At that time, India had very substantial trade with South Africa.

According to Indian statistics, India's exports to South Africa in 1944-1945 were valued at 119 million rupees, and imports from South Africa at 30 million rupees. South Africa accounted for 5.5 per cent of the total exports of India.

India recalled its High Commissioner in South Africa in 1946 and closed the High Commission in 1954.

India was one of the 34 co-sponsors of General Assembly resolution 1761 (XVII) of November 6, 1962, which requested Member States to implement a series of sanctions against South Africa. India then took further measures for full implementation of the resolution.

A press note by the Ministry of External Affairs of India, dated July 13, 1963, stated:

"Although India was the first country, as far back as 1946, to declare diplomatic and economic sanctions against South Africa, the Government of India has further reviewed the position and taken the necessary action to comply with resolution 1761 (XVII) of the United Nations. Some of the measures taken on the recommendations of the resolution are as follows:

"(a) Breaking off diplomatic relations with the government of the Republic of South Africa or refraining from establishing such relations.

"The High Commissioner for India in the Union of South Africa was recalled in 1946. The Mission itself was withdrawn in 1954. Thus, there has been no formal diplomatic connection between India and South Africa since 1954. However, some contact was maintained between the two Governments through their Missions in London, mainly in order to implement the various resolutions of the United Nations General Assembly, urging negotiations between them on the question of treatment of persons of Indian origin in South Africa. The Government of South Africa, however, persistently refused to negotiate in terms of these resolutions. This contact has accordingly now been broken off.

"(b) Closing ports to all vessels flying the South African flag." In implementation of resolution 1761 (XVII), the Government of India has instructed the authorities concerned not to allow vessels flying the South Africa flag to touch Indian seaports.

"(c) Enacting legislation prohibiting Indian ships from entering South African ports.

"Indian ships do not call at South African ports. However, instructions have been issued to the authorities concerned to prohibit Indian ships from going to the South African ports.

The Government of India has adequate powers for this purpose under the existing laws and it is not necessary to enact fresh legislation.

"(d) Boycotting all South African goods and refraining from exporting goods, including all arms and ammunition, to South Africa.

"There has been a general ban on the trade between India and South Africa since 1946. Since 1953, the mandated territory of South West Africa which is being administered by South Africa, has also been brought under this ban. The movement of some items, mainly of cultural and religious interest, was however, being allowed through postal and other channels on humanitarian grounds. The Government of India has examined this matter again and issued instructions that apart from bona fide personal effects of travellers, post-cards, letters, aerogrammes, and telegrams, only the following items will be allowed for movement between India and South Africa through postal and other channels:

(1) Books and periodicals, publications (magazines) and newspapers;

(2) Blind Literature;

(3) Free unsolicited gifts from relations and friends including family and personal photographs if paid for at the letter postage rates, or printed matter rates, if admissible. These cannot be sent by parcel post. The value of such gifts should not exceed Rs. 200.

(4) Packets containing sweetmeats and blessings for Muslim devotees by the Dargah Committee, Ajmer, provided that no packet exceeds one pound in weight and that packets are accompanied by certificates from the Nizam of the Dargah showing that they are bona fide offerings by devotees;

(5) Pictorial representations with religious and social background.

"(e) Refusing landings and passage facilities to all aircraft belonging to the Government of South Africa and companies registered under the laws of South Africa;

"There is no traffic between India and South Africa by Indian or South African airlines. However, under the relevant international conventions, aircraft registered in South Africa can be permitted to overfly India while operating scheduled international air services, to land at Indian airports for non-traffic purposes and to make non-scheduled flights to, through and over India. In view of the resolution of the General Assembly of the United Nations specifically forbidding these facilities, the Government of India has informed the International Civil Aviation Organisation that they will not allow aircraft registered in South Africa to land at Indian airports or to overfly India....

"The Government of India has, as explained above, implemented all the requirements of this resolution and hopes that all other Member States of the United Nations and indeed all countries of the world will do everything in their power to bring about the abandonment of the cruel and inhuman racial policies of the Government of South Africa."

ASSISTANCE TO THE OPPRESSED PEOPLE

India contributes to the United Nations fund for assistance to the victims of apartheid, to the Solidarity Fund of the Non-Aligned Movement for support to the African liberation movements, to the OAU Assistance Fund for the Struggle Against Colonialism and Apartheid and to the International Defence and Aid Fund for Southern Africa. It provides the technical training, education facilities and scholarships to a large number of South African and Namibian students.

Moreover, India has provided substantial material assistance to the ANC and the South West Africa People's Organisation (SWAPO).

The Asian Regional Office of the African National Congress of South Africa was opened in New Delhi with the financial assistance of the Government of India with Moosa Moolla, a veteran freedom fighter from South Africa as the first Representative of ANC. SWAPO was invited to establish an office some years later, and was given diplomatic status in 1985.

SPORTS AND CULTURAL BOYCOTT

India has also played an important role in the sports and cultural boycott of South Africa.

India does not allow apartheid sports teams and sports persons to play in India and Indian teams and sports persons do not play in South Africa. Indian sports bodies pressed prosposals in international sports bodies for the exclusion of South Africa.

Indian teams and competitors have boycotted sporting events to which South Africa was admitted. In 1974, for instance, the All-India Lawn Tennis Association officially refused to play South Africa in the Davis Cup Tennis finals, thus foregoing the possibility of championship.

Action by India was largely responsible for the decision by British cricket authorities to prohibit test cricketers from playing in South Africa.

India also supports the cultural boycott of South Africa and has dissuaded many entertainers from accepting lucrative offers from South Africa. Though this involves deprivation of cultural contacts to the people of Indian origin in South Africa, the Government has been firm in its policy.

OTHER MEASURES

India became a party to the International Convention on the Suppression and Punishment of the Crime of Apartheid in October, 1977. It enacted the Anti-Apartheid United Nations Convention Act, 1981, to give effect to the provisions of the International Convention.

India's support for the freedom struggle in South Africa was also demonstrated in other ways. For instance, the Jawaharlal Nehru Award for International Understanding for the year 1979 was conferred upon Nelson Mandela in recognition of his fight against oppression and race prejudice and in the cause of human brotherhood and equality.

AFRICA FUND

At the Harare Summit of NAM in 1986, Prime Mimister Rajiv Gandhi initiated the move to start the AFRICA Fund (AFRICA being an apt and significant acronym for "Action For Resisting Invasion, Colonialism and Apartheid).

It was constituted with India (Rajiv Gandhi) as Chairman. The other Members of the Executive Board are: Chadli Bendgedid (Algeria), Raul Ricardo Alfonsin (Argentina), Denis Sasson-Nguesso, Chairman, Organisation of African Unity (Congo), Ibrahim B. Babingida (Nigeria), Alan Garcia Perez (Peru), Sinan Hasani (Yugoslavia), Kenneth Kaunda, Chairman, Frontline States (Zambia) and Robert Mugabe, Chairman, Non-Aligned Movement (Zimbabwe).

India has pledged Rupees 500 million in kind to the Fund.

APPENDIX 7

Gandhiji's Important Message to South Africa

From *Passive Resister*, Johannesburg, May 30, 1947.

Dr. Y.M. Dadoo and Dr. G.M. Naicker, the South African Indian leaders stayed for two days with Mahatma Gandhi at Patna, before they left for South Africa and had full and frank talks covering the whole field of the political situation in South Africa.

The following message was given to South Africa through them by Mahatma Gandhi before their departure:

Field Marshal Smuts is a trustee for Western Civilisation. I still cling to hope that he will not sustain it on suppression of Asiatics and Africans. South Africa should at present be a blend of the three.

To European South Africans, to whom I am no stranger, I would say that they should not make the position of their representatives impossible by unwarranted prejudice against colour. The future is surely not with the so-called White race, if they keep themselves in "purdah."

That attitude of unreason will mean a third war, which all sane people should avoid.

Political cooperation among all exploited races in South Africa can only result in mutual good, if wisely directed.

To those South African Indians, who seem to create divisions, I say they will do harm to themselves and to the great cause of liberty for which the *Satyagraha* has stood and must stand.

170

To the Passive Resisters, I would advise strict adherence to the fundamentals of *Satyagraha*, which literally means force of truth and this is ever invincible. It is a good sign that they have progressive groups of Europeans solidly behind them.

The *Satyagrahis* of South Africa should know that they have India at their back in the struggle for preserving the self-respect of the Indians in South Africa.

ACKNOWLEDGMENTS

The Editor wishes to thank

1. The Prime Minister of India for his spirited message.

2. Mr. Eduardo Faleiro, Minister of State, External Affairs Government of India, for releasing this book at New Delhi on Oliver Tambo's 70th birthday on October 27, 1987.

3. Nikhil Chakravartty for all cooperation — and the preface.

4. Dr. Mulk Raj Anand for his enthusiastic support to the project

5. S.K. Ghai for undertaking to publish the book so readily.

6. Jag Mohan for being so involved in the book from planning to completion.

7. Moosa Moolla, Asian Regional Representative of ANC, Delhi for valuable help.

8. The Commonwealth Secretariat and Penguin Books, the Third World Foundation, Heinemann, London and Trustees of Vishwabharati University for allowing to reproduce texts for which they hold copyright.

9. Shaheed Prakashan Press for printing the book in record time.

10. K. Gopalakrishnan and D.D. Verma for secretarial assistance.